DO THE IMPOSSIBLE

BE CREATIVE have fun!

imaginate

Make some thing Beautiful

LIVE YOUR PURPOSE!

JOHN MICHAEL HINTON
in collaboration with KEN CASTOR

LET'S COLLAB!

Art is Essential

BroadStreet
P U B L I S H I N G

BroadStreet Publishing® Group, LLC
Savage, Minnesota, USA
BroadStreetPublishing.com

imaginate

Copyright © 2022 John Michael Hinton and Ken Castor

978-1-4245-6536-8 (softcover)
978-1-4245-6537-5 (e-book)

Stock or custom editions of BroadStreet Publishing titles may be purchased in bulk for educational, business, ministry, fundraising, or sales promotional use. For information, please email orders@broadstreetpublishing.com.

Illustrations by Maribeth Hinton, Ken Castor & John Michael Hinton
Cover by Maribeth Hinton & Garborg Design Works
Interior by Garborg Design Works | garborgdesign.com

Printed in China.

22 23 24 25 26 5 4 3 2 1

ENDORSEMENTS

John has collected in these pages ideas for your life that are both practical and winsome. He takes you on a delightful ride using relatable stories about real life and real faith. You are really going to enjoy this book.

Bob Goff
Author, *New York Times* bestsellers *Love Does*, *Everybody Always*, and *Dream Big*

John Michael has been a friend of ours for several years, and we've been huge fans of everything he does. *imaginate* inspires us to keep pushing the boundaries of what we can do creatively together. You've got to devour this book.

Tommy Woodard and Eddie James
The SkitGuys

John Michael's themes of purposeful creativity and art speak to me deeply, and I'm inspired by his urge toward collaboration and community. The openness with which he shared sacred moments from his life to illustrate these ideas is moving. I can't wait to take these thoughts and apply them to my own life's work!

Mario "The Maker Magician" Marchese
Performer, Author, Creator

These two dudes are the real deal! I've loved working with John Michael Hinton and Ken Castor at next-gen conferences all over the US. And now I'm pumped that they've written a really fun, refreshing book that sparks the creative process in all of us. *imaginate* is the inspirational collision of two resilient creatives who encourage people to thrive even when difficulties get in the way. I can't wait to see what good things God is going to do when people imaginate!

Josh Griffin
Speaker; Youth Pastor; Co-founder, DownloadYouthMinistry.com

My experience is that all too often, people overcomplicate creativity, making it into something they can either claim or distance themselves from. But John Michael and Ken reminded me (over and over again, actually) of truths about God, myself, and creativity that are quite literally woven into my design (and yours, by the way). At its heart, this encouraging book is an invitation not only to collab and imaginate with God and others but also to see yourself how God sees you.

Mark Oestreicher
Founder and Partner, The Youth Cartel

What are the first five words of the Bible? "In the beginning God..." Copyright infringed? Plagiarized? Duplicated? Nope: "In the beginning God *created!*" Imagine you could imitate an artist like that. The first of the firsts. *imaginate* will put the path in front of you and some very practical tools in your hands. This is a must-read for anyone who makes anything from spreadsheets to suspension bridges to spit wads.

Eric Samuel Timm
Artist, Author, Pastor

Pre-*imaginate*, I felt like I had a pretty whole and accurate view of our creative God. Nope. I didn't. Post-*imaginate*, I see a God who laughed while creating and delights in collaborating with me in unique and fun ways! If I were in charge of coordinating a creative round table, John Michael would be my first pick! (Walt Disney my second.) His take on everyday life and the God who invited us into that everyday life is fresh, fun, and fascinating! Every one of my students needs to be shaped and grounded by the perspective on God's creativity revealed in this book. John Michael's personal story, told with such humor and detail, intersects masterfully and insightfully with God's story. *imaginate* is more than temporary art—it's here to stay!

Heather Flies
Junior High Pastor, Wooddale Church, Eden Prairie

For the creative person, maybe coloring outside the lines is normal. But for all those who have never experienced the wonder of a Broadway show, nor awed at a masterful magician expanding their imagination, this book has enough mystery to make everyone want to run for the crayons. Thank you, John and Ken, for ensuring none of us ever see the creation story, nor a deck of cards, the same way again. Thanks for helping us *imaginate*!

Jonathan Meyer
Pastor; Founder, Ignite Youth Leadership Conferences

One of my greatest thrills in life is to help people discover the unlimited love and life that God offers to everyone. There's nothing quite like living in the fullness of life that God has creatively and uniquely set before each of us. *imaginate* helps us to tap into that life of joy, hope, and wonder. This book is an eye-awakening, soul-inspiring, super-fun deep-dive into the creative work that God has for us.

Zane Black
Evangelist; Founder, wearelovinlife.com

Over the years, I've come to see John Michael Hinton as someone who does the incredible in a way I just cannot understand. I love watching him perform, and I have no idea how he does his illusions or what the hidden trick might be. But in *imaginate*, he is all about the opposite—he actually breaks open the deep mysteries of life and Scripture and, through his personal story, reveals the details of God's imaginative invitation to create. This is an inspiring and great read for anyone.

Scott Wakely
National Director, Alliance Youth, LIFE Conference

When John and Ken, two of my most creative and coolest friends, get together to write a book, you know something amazing is going to happen. They've taken the best of their passions and stories and mashed them into fun adventures and deep discoveries about the very essence of life. John and Ken know that people truly thrive when they connect with God and others. I'm excited to see how *imaginate* will spark movements of creativity that change the world.

Brad Mock
High School Pastor, Christ Community Church, Omaha

As a magician myself, I understand the special gift John Michael Hinton has given us here. Good magicians want to help people marvel at the world, expand their sense of wonder, and help them imagine new possibilities. With the help of a trusted voice in Ken Castor, John has crafted a masterpiece for the soul that changes how we approach our lives. *imaginate* is an entertaining invitation into a secret world...a world inhabited as it was meant to be: with abundant wisdom and humor and awe.

Mark Matlock
Author; Consultant; Principal and Founder, Wisdom Works

TABLE OF CONTENTS

INTRODUCTION

imaginate

I envision a round table with the most creative minds dreaming and brainstorming together all committed to bringing a beautiful idea into reality. They've been commissioned to create an amazing art piece that will express the deepest of truths and that will inspire others to be the best versions of themselves. If you're anything like me, you want a seat at that table.

The best hope for humankind is when humans do what they were designed to do: operate in a collaborative existence with our Creator and each other, using the unique gifts we were given to artistically craft our world into a better version for every generation after us.

When I'm not playing with my kids on the living room floor or drinking large cups of black tea with my wife, you'll find me making videos for my socials or trekking around the world speaking at retreats and performing magic shows. Over and over, I'm amazed and humbled at the platform I have to share my story and make new friends. Whether on large stages or in small groups of friends, my desire is to impact this world by bringing good things to life.

But, transparently, I often feel like I'm not capable or worthy or skilled enough to be at a table engaged with imaginative, productive people. My psychologist friends tell me I have a very common problem among creatives called "impostor syndrome." This feeling of insecurity sabotages my ability to see a dream through to reality. This feeling overwhelms me most when I compare myself to other creatives and influencers. There is always someone more talented, more fashionable, more mature, or more widely known than me. And then I feel like trash.

Do you ever feel that way?

But...

...what if we were not trash? What if God not only enjoyed creating us but also delights in recreating us? As a great artist, what if God created mankind as his "self-portrait." In his likeness, his image. What if we were endowed with his breath, his character, and his creative calling?

My hope for you as you read this book is that you will embrace your value and the value of what you have to give this world. I want you to discover the joy of journeying through the creative collaborative process. It's a journey you were created to take. Designed to take. I can't wait to hear the stories of all of you who join God's invitation to collab with him as he brings back beauty and art to our fractured world.

imaginate
verb
/im`ag´i`nate/
To create imaginatively in collaboration

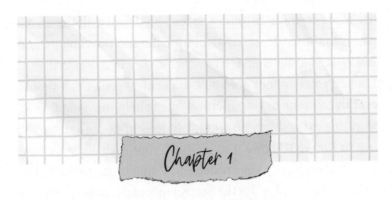

"IT MUST HAVE BEEN FUN!"

I accumulate a ton of airline miles. My job, which primarily involves motivational speaking and doing magic shows,[1] takes me all over this great world. In one stretch recently, I traveled first to Erie, Pennsylvania, then to St. Cloud, Minnesota, then to St. Croix, Wisconsin, then to Charlotte, North Carolina. I was home for ten days until I went back on the road to Fremont, Nebraska, then to Littleton, Colorado, then to Hilton Head, South Carolina, then to Pittsburgh, Pennsylvania. You get the idea.

When I first started traveling, one of my mentors told me, "John, the road is hard! Being away from your family is really hard. So you always have to find a way to make road life fun." This has become my mantra on the road. Whether it's trying a cool local restaurant or buying a nosebleed ticket to a ball game, I now always try to "make road life fun." But one of the main ways I accomplish this is by saving up my airline miles so that I can go on fun adventures with my family.

One time, after I had accumulated over two hundred thousand miles,[2] I told my wife she could pick anywhere in

---

1   See www.johnismyfriend.com for all the awesome details of my world. :)

2   The moon is 238,900 miles away from the earth. I could make frequent

the world to travel to, and we'd go. She debated all the exotic places in the world, scoured all the Pinterest travel blogs, and finally landed on Rome. And what a wise decision that was! Look, if you have not been able to decide whether you should ever fly to Rome in your lifetime, let me help you—*do it*! Save, work the extra shifts, do what you need to do, and make the trip to Rome. You owe it to yourself, your eyeballs, your nostrils, and especially your tastebuds. Rome is one of the oldest cities in the world and is the perfect mix of the historic and the modern, creating one of the greatest cities that is always full of life. We ate all the pizza, pasta, and gelato we could and fit in as many historical sites until we were blissfully exhausted.

And while we were there, we made sure to visit one of the biggest tourist destinations on earth: the Sistine Chapel.

Honestly, my wife was more excited to visit it than I was. I know it's the pope's chapel. I know the legendary artist Michelangelo painted his masterpiece on the ceiling and altar. But let me shamefully admit my ignorance and vanity here. I have traveled a lot. I have seen many of the great wonders of the world, been to many of the great art museums of the world, and had the privilege to stand in front of and take in with my own eyes many famous works of art. From Leonardo's *Mona Lisa* to Rembrandt's *Prodigal Son* to the best velvet Elvis paintings in Mexico's flea markets, I've seen tons of famous paintings and spent time in famous art museums all over the world. For instance, while living in Paris, France, I would frequently just hang out in the world's largest art museum, the Louvre,[3] go get a ham and cheese baguette sandwich, and pop

---

flier trips to the moon. The earth is 24,901 miles in circumference. I could fly around the world ten times on frequent flier miles.

3   Most English-speaking people have no clue how to say this word. Does this help? /ˈluːv(ɹə)/.

over to the Notre Dame Cathedral to listen to a choir practice or just enjoy the peacefulness in one of the chapels.

Yes, I've been spoiled. Yes, you guessed it, I may have become a little bit jaded. Yes, I know the Sistine Chapel had a "master" painter paint on the ceiling. And yes, it has been featured in countless art books, on T-shirts, on keychains, and memes. I knew I should be excited about visiting this legendary site. But I was like: "Uh, really, another chapel? I mean I guess we are here, but then let's see what else is cool to do around here. When in Rome, right?"

I was simply wrong.

when in Rome...
- GO GET GELATO!
- STARE AT THE SISTINE CHAPEL CEILING UNTIL YOUR NECK HURTS
- VISIT THE COLOSSEUM AND OTHER OLD RUINED STUFF
- EAT PIZZA
- EAT **MORE** GELATO!
- RIDE A VESPA
- DRINK A MORNING CAPPUCCINO
- EAT MORE ITALIAN FOOD
- EAT GELATO FOR DESSERT!
- MEET THE POPE
- FIND A GELATO SHOP WITH A LINE OUT THE DOOR. GET IN LINE!

Before we went to Rome, a good friend gave us the tip to get "early admission" to the chapel. It's a little more money, and you have to wake up way too early (which is a real problem for two night owl creatives whose bedtime is normally between two and three in the morning. And did I mention we were jet lagged?). But we will be forever grateful for this advice.

We woke up at 4:45 a.m. to catch an Uber to the Vatican City. Standing out in the cold, we found our tour group and showed them our passes. With only about fifty other people (which is way different from the mobs of hundreds or thousands that you would normally be with), we were ushered through the halls leading up to the chapel. I'm not a mean guy. I like making friends. But I was tired, impatient, and wishing we could speed this process up. The cappuccinos and gelato cafes of Rome were beckoning me elsewhere.

Once inside, however, I knew I had been a fool. The halls leading up to the chapel surprised my apathetic thoughts. All of a sudden, my attitude had changed from "let's-get-this-over-with" to "hold-on-this-is-amazing!" The ancient corridors, lined by huge intricate tapestries, were awe-inspiring. And we weren't even to the chapel yet. Someday, I want to visit this incredible place again simply to slow down in the halls to be able to take in all the art. But our tour group had momentum moving us forward. We were on a mission—to see the great Sistine Chapel.

But even then, I wavered. Right before the chapel, there is a bit of an obstacle. As if to say to the sojourner, "Are you sure you're ready for this?" A test of the will is issued. Just outside the chapel, there is a humble, narrow, circular staircase that challenges the determination of any cynical, spoiled pilgrim like me. In fact, the stairs reminded me of what I have affectionately called my "fat man squeeze" that I have experienced while exploring caves. I had to press on, down into the cavern of this massive, ancient building, bumping my shoulders against the walls, spiraling down the uneven stairs. With each descending step onto each stone stair, my expectation went down as well.

But then we stepped into the chapel.

It was as if someone hooked up a shop vacuum to each of my lungs and turned it on full blast. Every last bit of oxygen was sucked from my lungs. My breath was literally taken away.

I had seen many pictures of the different works of Michelangelo in books. But just like seeing a two-dimensional picture of a sunset versus experiencing it with your own eyes while sitting on Newport Beach with the waves of the Pacific Ocean lapping in front of you…I had no idea how incredible it could be.

Another valuable tip we received from our friend was to download the "Rick Steve's Audio Guide to the Sistine Chapel." (You could make an argument that Rick Steve is kind of like the Michelangelo of tour guides.) This audio guide explains to your ears the when, how, and why of every bit of art displayed before your eyes. It helps you unpack every detail of this incredible masterpiece through the lens of an expert. We sat and allowed the guide to explain to us the different parts of the massive art piece. I was astonished at the considerable amount of work put into the six days of the creation story from the book of Genesis that were depicted in the middle of the chapel ceiling.

It took Michelangelo four years to complete this massive project. There are nine central scenes at the top of the ceiling. These scenes are surrounded by dozens of other panels and depictions. The most famous scene, the *Creation of Adam*, (you know, the part that is featured in all the formerly mentioned books, T-shirts, and memes) is the painting of the white-haired, stoic God reaching out to touch the finger of the man. For the next two and a half hours my wife and I marveled until we started getting neck cramps from staring at the ceiling so long.

Picture of God and Adam from Sistine Chapel[4]

And then my wife blew my mind with simply a statement.
She leaned over to me and said, "Must have been fun."
I leaned back and said, "Yeah…what?"
"Creating all this."
"Yeah…wait…what do you mean?"
"God. Creating the world…it must have been fun for him."
Then my mind melted.
A story I thought I knew so well took on a whole new light.
When I had read the words of the creation story in Genesis, I always pictured God the Father as Michelangelo had painted him. Just one stern old guy with an admittedly

---

4   I took this picture (I might have been a rebel with all the signs posted not to…but I took it).

majestic beard, giving out orders of what should be done. "Let there be light…let there be water…let there be fish, animals, humans." Like a captain barking out orders to his crew. After God did all this, I just always thought that he must have sat down, stroked his serious beard on his stern face, and decided that he earned a rest on the seventh day. Stoic. Impassive.

Phlegmatic.

Phlegmatic[5] is a word I learned recently. This disgusting sounding word describes someone who has an "absence of interest" or a "lack of curiosity" or a "void of responsiveness." I'm embarrassed to say that I guess I just always pictured God as phlegmatic toward what he had made.

But this statement of my wife's—"Must have been fun."

What if…

It was completely different?

What if the way I pictured it…

Was all wrong?

What if God was in his zone as an artist when he was making the world? How great did he feel? What if after six flurry-filled days of sculpting and painting and constructing and designing God…stopped.

Stepped back…and smiled.

Like an artist who, after finishing something he is particularly proud of, turns the canvas to reveal his work to a trusted friend.

In the Genesis account, we are told that after creating all the things each day, God stopped and said, "It is good."

How do you hear God saying those words? I always pictured a big, Morgan Freeman in *Shawshank Redemption,* serious voice booming from the clouds, "*It. Is. Good.*"

---

5   Phlegmatic /fleg'madik/.

But what if instead…

God created…stepped back…paused.

And smiled.

Can you picture God nudging some of the angels who were trying to get a good look over those massive God-shoulders? And what if God, with a small, joyful laugh, then stood back, opened his arms to the angels, and unveiled what he had made. "It is good!"

Perhaps God said, "Check it out, Gabriel! We created light! Do you see all those different colors? And, look, when you bend it like this (pulling out a God-sized prism), it causes refraction, and all the different colors dance around on the land and water…well, when there *is* land and water…oh just wait a couple days and see!"

"Michael! You have to come see this. Notice how the waters flow all around but stop at the land? Do you see how some of the waters stop by sand and others by rocky cliffs? Oh, and the sea is salty, but the rivers, even though they are connected to the ocean, they stay sweet. *Ha!* It's *good!*"

"Look at these plants! This one we are hiding deep in this amazon of a jungle just for us. No one else will ever discover this. Oh, and this tree…We are making it so it will be ever-green, almost like a birthday present for Jesus. Ha!"

"And these other trees…they will signify the changing of the seasons by changing the color of their leaves—creating a whole new temporary art piece every year until they drop their leaves to create fertilizer for other things to grow."

"Clarence,[6] check out these fish! From this smallest swimmer to this giant, big blue whale of one. Ha! Oh, and in

---

6   *It's a Wonderful Life* fans? My wife wanted me to point out that Clarence would not have been at creation as he lived when the book *Tom Sawyer* by Mark Twain came out…and that he only got his wings after his

the deepest parts, we are going to give this scary one a little light attached by a little hangy-downy thing to his head so he can see and attract prey. Look! Do you see? It's good!"

"And these flying animals? Clarence, they've got their wings! We are making their bones hollow and giving them beautiful feathers on their arms so they can instinctually know how to navigate the wind currents, using them to turn and glide in the skies. Are you looking? It's *good*!"

"Hey, everyone! Check out these animals walking along the earth. We're going to make most of them wild and ferocious. Right? Creating a circle of life. But we're also going to make some of them to be pets.[7] So, the wolf and dog will be related, but one will hunt, and one will just want to play fetch and have this cute little head turning thing when he doesn't quite understand you. Oh, it's good!"

"But *wait*! Now let's do something really fun…"

And what if at that moment, all the angels leaned in as they jockeyed to be able to see?

And what if God picked up some dust and earth and, as so many artists that would come after, said, "Now let's make a self-portrait."

And right before the angels' eyes, like the first, and greatest, sculptor ever, using this medium at his disposal, God created this…this…this human. The Hebrew word here is *adamah*. Literally, "earth/dirt man." A man created from the dirt of the earth.

And then visualize how God did something new to this earth-man that he hadn't done with the rest of his living

---

interaction with George Bailey in 1945.

7   That's straight out of Genesis 1:24, by the way. Serious! God made pets different from wild beasts on purpose for us. So crazy!

creatures: God cradled this creation's face in his gentle hands and breathed his very own breath of life into Adam's nostrils.

Then God stepped back and pointed and said to the audience,

"Now. *That*. Is. *Really*. Good."

Masterpiece.

The. Greatest. Artwork. Ever.

It must have been fun.

ABOUT THE ARTIST

The first thing God tells us about himself is that he is an artist. A creator.

The very first words of Scripture reveal this. That's kind of a big deal. Down the line, if you were going to start your message for humanity—you know, the message that would help all those wandering descendants of Adam rediscover you and find their way back to you—you would need a good "hook." You'd need something that would get people's attention. Something that would make them take notice...to pause and look. Something that would stir a sense of wonder.

So God decided to start his message this way:

"In the beginning God *created* the heavens and the earth."[8]

"God *created*" is the foundational starting point for the purpose and experience of every single human being. Without this, there are no trees or lakes. There are no mountains. There are no deep-dish pizzas. Without God first creating, there would be no *us*! And there would be nothing for us to create *with*.

---

8   Genesis 1:1, NLT (emphasis added).

We create because God first created.

Don't miss that. Don't take that for granted.

It's not like God said, "Well, since I don't have any internet reception, I guess I'll make something today." God wasn't just lounging around with a bag of chips bored out of his mind, looking for something to take up his time. "Yawn. Let's see, what should I do today? I suppose I could go to the annual angel egg roll fundraiser...again."[9] No, God is creative. Literally. God is not bound by the confines of space and time[10] and material. He took a void and made things. Without a palette of pre-existing material, without space and without time, out of nothing, God created.

And with that hook, God helps us realize that we are mere time travelers and space explorers in constant wonder of an unfathomably remarkable Creator.

The second verse of Scripture describes a scene where God, the master artist, prepares to tackle a blank canvas with brilliant, creative abandon. God's anticipation is evident. He is energetic and ready. God was not going to restrain himself. Something amazing was about to happen:

"The earth was formless and empty, and darkness covered the deep waters. And the Spirit of God was hovering over the surface of the waters."[11]

Have you ever stood in front of a blank canvas with brush in hand? The possibilities of what the painting could be are infinite. Anything can be imagined. I love how God takes

---

9   Although an angel egg roll fundraiser sounds heavenly. No deviled eggs allowed though.

10   I got the following phrases, "not bound by the confines of space and time" and "pre-existing material" from J. I. Packer, *Concise Theology* (Carol Stream, IL: Tyndale, 1993), 21.

11   Genesis 1:2, NLT.

us to that moment before anything was made, when he stood back and took the time to *imaginate* what the world would be.

The canvas.

Formless.

Empty.

It was time for the artist's first brush stroke, the sculptor's first chisel, the architect's first line:

"Then God said, 'Let there be light' and there was light."[12]

It is so easy to read over those words and not really realize what is happening.

Because we have always had...

Light.

We don't know anything other than a world that has light. Can you imagine the universe without light? Not a chance. If you don't remember a time-before-something-existed, you can't grasp the concept of what it must have been like.

BL and AL. Before Light. After Light.

And now you just take it for granted.

But there was a time when there were no stars. No sun. No reflections of moons. No lightning storms. No candles. No fireflies. No digital screens. No neon "Eat Here Get Gas" roadside signs.

Light.

Let this idea be illuminated in your soul.

God *created* light.

Light is literally the agent that stimulates human sight and makes things visible. Science tells us that light is made of up ten million colors (and even more if you count the colors not visible to the human eye).

---

12   Genesis 1:3, NLT.

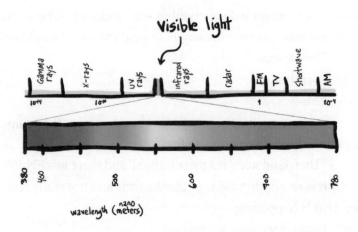

So not only does God first tell us he is a creator, but he also tells us that he is an artist. A creative. *The* Creative. The First Creative. The beginner of all creation. The handcrafter of every-thing…enjoying the process and not rushing over any detail.

By shedding light on the subject, God illuminates his creative work. God doesn't just tell us the *what* of creation, but he also wants us to see the *how*. He takes us on the journey of his creation and shows us the mediums he used to hand-craft each part. As if he were giving us his behind-the-scenes commentary (you know, the kind that all of us movie geeks love to get with the extended edition downloads), God walks us through the making of his masterpiece. God shows us his inventive process, day by day, imagination made real, creative endeavor after endeavor, until the full palette of life on earth as we know it takes shape.

He said, "Let there be light." And there was.

God created.

And he wants you to know his creative process.

I don't know how familiar you are with the first two chap-ters of the Bible, but I really think you'd find them fascinating.

Not only is the whole portfolio of God's creative process incredibly artistic, but so is the way that he communicates it to us.

But I've got to tell you, this is where our English language just falls a bit short.[13]

The first two chapters of Scripture tell us of the "genesis" of the world. Chapter 1 gives us a ten-thousand-foot bird's-eye-view of all of creation. And chapter 2 gives us a magnified glimpse into the human origin.

But unless you know ancient Hebrew, you could totally miss an incredible aspect of the creation account. You could easily miss that the first two chapters of the Bible are written in two beautiful and intentional literary forms that are meant to draw you in and personalize the experience for you: poetry and prose poetry.

Using these literary art forms for the first two chapters is like an invitation to the original round table of creativity. These first words reveal God at work, intentionally crafting humankind with his collaborative brilliance. And these first words offer us a commissioning to join in the process.

This is not an aloof story. This is not just an interesting tale. This is not a manual for us to use to fix a problem. This is not an encyclopedia to give humans control of information. This is poetry and prose, beckoning humanity to join God in a creative, collaborative relationship.

Of all the literary genres, only a poetic approach can fully describe the artistic, collaborative calling depicted here. With a free-flowing thought process, creation's beauty is

---

13 It seems to me that English most definitely is a language that results from the fall of Adam and Eve in Genesis chapter 3 or the confusion of the Tower of Babel in chapter 10. English has so many rules, and yet it seems like we're supposed to ignore half of them. Like *i* before *e* except when your foreign neighbor Keith receives eight counterfeit beige sleights from feisty caffeinated weightlifters. So weird.

highlighted. These chapters were not written like a textbook. They were written in a way to make you ponder, think, wonder, *imaginate*. It's as if God is pointing out to us, "Do you see how innovative creation is?"

And what does that reveal about your Creator?

And what does that reveal about you?

Now this might freak some people out. Some anxious people have worried and some narrow-minded people have speculated that if these first chapters were written as a poem and poetic prose, then it could mean that their depiction is just fiction. Is the Genesis account of creation just some flowery limerick?

We're constantly discovering the science of this world. People will be long gone before the full origin of humanity is fully understood in textbook detail. We will never exhaust the depths of wonder embedded into God's creative process.

And we will never exhaust the depths of description written into God's gallery exhibit.

Creatives speak with flair.

God, the Creative, speaks with flair and truth.

Some have argued that Genesis uses poetry and poetic prose as just a fun way to explain the creation of the world. They say the writer was trying to communicate in a simple way and never meant to be taken literally. But I think it is deeper than that. Just because something is written in poetic or poetic prose form doesn't determine whether it is fiction or nonfiction.

How many poems or pieces of poetic prose have you read about actual events? There are so many. Some have lost their power on us because we stop at the literary form and don't dare to look deeper.

Why do people sometimes choose to use poetry and prose poetry to relay essential truth as opposed to just a textbook historical account? The answer is quite simple actually: So that people will remember.

It is creative nonfiction.[14]

The creation story was passed down for generations until Moses wrote it down while Israel was enslaved in Egypt. First, it was passed down from generation to generation through Israel's oral tradition. Long before people kept books and libraries, long before printing presses and twenty-four-hour news outlets, the elders would tell important stories over and over in a communal setting so their history would not be forgotten. One of the best ways to communicate a vital event of this magnitude and keep all the details was via poetry.

Remember this one?

And the rocket's red glare,
The bombs bursting in air,
Gave proof through the night
That our flag was still there.

For well over two hundred years, generations have known the details of the bombardment of Fort McHenry by British ships during the War of 1812 because of Francis Scott Key's famous poem, which became our national anthem.

America.

An important origin story.

Earth.

A *more* important origin story.

14　Thanks Dr. Don Bouchard at Crown College for this description and for being a grammatical guru.

So, with an event of such epic magnitude, the creation story was passed down via poetic prose so we would keep the important details intact.

Also, perhaps God used creative language for the creation story to show us in yet another way how artistic he is. People in our contemporary western world seem to complain that Genesis doesn't give us a dry historical account of the facts of creation. But why would an artist have to explain the process of his masterpiece in dry technical terms? Can you imagine God's message to us sounding like a textbook? "When the mitochondria external membrane associates with the endoplasmic reticulum…"; "It is customary for the nocturnal ornithorhynchus semiaquatic, which is endemic to…"

Maybe the Google side of our inquisitive human nature would love to have that kind of detail, with photographic and video accounts, of course. To understand everything until we can control it and twist the wonder of creation to our advantage. This is certainly not to put down science in any way. The scientific discovery behind the why is also a gift God gave us and is so very important for us to understand.

But that's not how God wants to start. That's not what he first wants us to "see." God wants us to look and see that what he has made is "very good." God wants us to have a sense of wonder. Being an artist, God wants us to be drawn in to the artwork and mesmerized by the masterpiece. He invites us to be in awe of his ingenuity and cleverness. By communicating in poetry and poetic prose, the first chapters of Genesis cause us to marvel at all the creativity exhibited in creation.

God, an artist describing his art, reveals his process with flavor and conceptual prose:

- "Let there be a space between the waters, to separate the waters of the heavens from the waters of the earth…God called this space 'sky.' "[15]
- "Let lights appear in the sky to separate the day from the night. Let them be signs to mark the seasons, days, and years."[16]
- "Let the waters swarm with fish and other life. Let the skies be filled with birds of every kind."[17]
- "On the seventh day God had finished his work of creation, so he rested from all his work."[18]
- "The LORD God made all sorts of trees grow up from the ground—trees that were beautiful and that produced delicious fruit."[19]
- "While the man slept, the LORD God took out one of the man's ribs and closed up the opening. Then the LORD God made a woman from the rib, and he brought her to the man."[20]

That's not a textbook. That's an artist's description. Imagine going to the gallery to meet the creator in person and asking, "How did you make that amazing piece?" Genesis itself says that these first two chapters of the Bible are an "account of the creation of the heavens and the earth."[21] If you haven't figured it out yet, they are an account of a very imaginative, collaborative, and creative God.

---

15 Genesis 1:6–8, NLT.
16 Genesis 1:14, NLT.
17 Genesis 1:20, NLT.
18 Genesis 2:2, NLT.
19 Genesis 2:9, NLT.
20 Genesis 2:21–22, NLT.
21 Genesis 2:4, NLT.

And he wrote down what he wants us to know about his art.

So get in line and get your book signed.

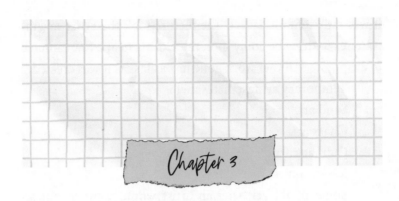

TEMPORARY ART

While walking from Space Mountain to the Dumbo ride with my family at Walt Disney World, we were stopped in our tracks. A large crowd that had gathered at the edge of Tomorrow Land drew our curiosity. The crowd stood in awe. To our surprise, they had been captivated and were watching...a janitor. With a bucket of water.

Over and over this guy would take his broom, which had been tightly tied together with plastic strings to form a giant brush, and dip it in the bucket of water. Then he would use the water to draw on the street. As he drew more and more lines the art piece revealed itself and we realized that he was drawing none other than the mouse himself, Mickey!

This is not a random occurrence at the Disney parks. Go ahead. Google it—"Disney janitor art." You will discover image after image of every Disney character: Mickey, Donald, Goofy, Simba, and even Mike Wazowski from *Monsters, Inc.*, sketched with liquid by the Disney janitors.

As we watched the artist draw with water, we were mesmerized. It was beyond cool, and it lasted in our memory. Yet it was only temporary art. The picture took the artist several minutes to draw but only took the Florida heat a few minutes to evaporate. All that work gone just as fast as it was created.

Temporary art fascinates me!

Sand art.

Chalk art.

Culinary art.

Ice sculptures.

Some might ask why an artist would want to put so much time and effort into something when the elements and/or time will so quickly destroy all the hard work. And yet temporary art can often be the most special and spectacular. It can only be viewed for a very short time by the select few who are present at the exact time it is happening, and it can never be recreated exactly the same again.

This concept really hit me when I performed at the J&B Magic Theater in New Albany, Indiana. This theater, located ten minutes from downtown Louisville, Kentucky, and run by my friend Brent Braun, is a small, close-up magic venue with only thirty-two seats. At the beginning of every show Brent explains the history of the building. He gives every audience the same lesson:

> This place where you sit used to be a twenty-five-hundred-seat opera house, but in 1939, there was a horrible fire that consumed the entire building. Though the building was rebuilt, at the same time just down the street, a new type of entertainment had opened where these pictures would move like magic. The new building was called a "movie theater." As a result, this opera house lost its patrons and had to

close down. The building was dissected into other businesses and stores. And, yet, tonight, all of you have come together looking for a distraction from those screens. To be able to experience live entertainment in this place yet again.

All live performance is temporary art. Most of my magic shows are the same series of tricks, and yet, depending on how audience members interact and react to things, each show is a different adventure every time. In the same way, you could attend all eight shows that a Broadway musical in New York performs in a week, and, though it is the same script, music, and actors, every show would be slightly different in the unique moment of time. Every song sung before a live audience is an extraordinary instant. Every fireworks display is a brilliant one-time flash in the night. Every flower garden is seasonal.

God treasures those unique experiences.

God loves temporary art!

Just look up at the clouds.

The vivid artistry of the sky leaves us in awe.

There are more than one hundred different types of clouds.[22] What? That's why the old childhood pastime of lying in a grassy field on your back and staring up at the clouds is always new. From dragons, to pirate ships, to puppy dogs, we can let our imaginations run wild and discover new worlds every day simply by looking up.

And we haven't even touched the idea of what happens to these clouds at dawn and dusk. These puffy white and grey

---

22 According to the World Meteorological Organization's International Cloud Atlas, https://cloudatlas.wmo.int/en/cloud-classification-summary.html.

mists become a colorful, ever-changing display of wonder. Sunsets are simply incredible, right? And the unique view is brand new and different every day in every location on earth. Diversity of wind patterns, atmospheric pressures, temperatures, and geographies cause an infinite set of variables. Every canvas of the sky is a masterpiece...God collaborating yet again, showing off his artistic brush to create again and again.

As mentioned before, one of the perks of my magic/speaking career is that I get to fly a lot. After take-off, I love to open the plane window shade and stare out at the clouds. The large cumulus clouds, the wisps of cirrus clouds, the frightful mammatus formations drooping beneath thunder clouds. All of these masses of condensed water vapor, visible to the human eye, just defying gravity and floating in the atmosphere absolutely fill me with wonder. To the person in the plane seat next to me, who may have already been concerned about my orange jet-fueled hair, I probably look like a little kid jaw-dropped in awe.

But one day of flying in particular stands above the rest. It was dusk. The light was fading, and, for some reason, the window shade had been pulled shut. From around the edges of the shade, I saw something I had never seen before—a brilliant pink hue framing the window. It looked like one of those LED strips you might put behind a TV or around the walls of your room. Intrigued, I opened the shade and saw what must have been twenty hues of pink out in the sky. Honestly, at first this confused me. It even worried me a bit. Why were we surrounded by all this pink? Every disaster movie scenario went through my mind. Was there a nuclear war I didn't know about? Was there a cotton candy factory on fire thousands of feet below? Had we entered into my little girl's dream world of pink? Then it hit me—and it was the most amazing thing my eyes had ever seen—we were flying *through* a sunset! As time went on, the pink colors morphed into dark reds and purples. There were hints of maroon and streaks of blazing orange. I marveled in silence, having no words to express the beauty. I wanted it to continue forever. But the colors of this unique canvas eventually faded, replaced by night scattered with stars across the dimming sky.

And this process repeats anew *every* night.

In all parts of the globe.

3 THOUSAND years ago ANOTHER CREATIVE PERSON → DAVID WROTE THESE WORDS ABOUT THE CREATION'S RELATIONSHIP *with the creator...*

GOD'S SPLENDOR IS A TALE THAT IS TOLD,
WRITTEN IN THE STARS.
SPACE ITSELF SPEAKS HIS STORY
THROUGH THE MARVELS OF THE HEAVENS.
HIS TRUTH IS ON TOUR IN THE STARRY VAULT OF THE SKY,
SHOWING HIS SKILL IN CREATION'S CRAFTSMANSHIP.
EACH DAY GUSHES OUT ITS MESSAGE TO THE NEXT,
NIGHT BY NIGHT WHISPERING ITS KNOWLEDGE TO ALL—
WITHOUT A SOUND, WITHOUT A WORD,
WITHOUT A VOICE BEING HEARD,
YET ALL THE WORLD CAN HEAR ITS ECHO.
EVERYWHERE ITS MESSAGE GOES OUT.
WHAT A HEAVENLY HOME GOD HAS SET FOR THE SUN,
SHINING IN THE SUPERDOME OF THE SKY!

And on this earth, for his enjoyment and ours, every day God stretches out a new canvas on which to paint happy little clouds, and every day he wipes it clean to replace it with a nighttime canvas.

And that's not where it ends. From how the wind shapes a sand dune, to how sunlight refracts off raindrops to form a rainbow, even to how a wave forms in seconds just to crash onto the shore, God delights in creating and recreating every minute, second, and nano-second.

God's continual desire for creating temporary art demonstrates that whether it is something as long-lasting as a mountain or as temporary as ripples forming across a lake, God will never be finished with his creative work. The Scriptures promise that even after we die, God has plans for a new heaven, new earth, and even a new body for us.[23]

Just as "in the beginning," God will not restrain himself and his creative pursuits by time, space, or material, and even though we are but a whisper in comparison to his permanence, he treasures the opportunity to create and collab with us.

---

23 Revelation 21:1.

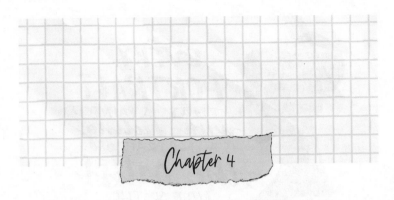

A COLLABORATIVE SELF-PORTRAIT

Have you ever tried to sketch or paint a self-portrait? Pretty difficult. The toughest thing is you know exactly what you look like, and so does everybody else. Self-portraits are not mirrors. They are instead expressions of how artists see themselves. Colorful, dingy, with or without the pimples[24] are all an artistic decision based on how the artist is feeling when looking in the mirror.

We are God's self-portrait.

Think about that for a second. God's self-portrait.

It's the first thing we find out about humankind.

Created in the "image of God."

Made "like God."

In Likeness.

In Being.

In Purpose.

A divine self-portrait.

---

24 "When I did my self-portrait, I left all the pimples out because you always should. Pimples are a temporary condition and they don't have anything to do with what you really look like. Always omit the blemishes—they're not part of the good picture you want." Andy Warhol, *The Philosophy of Andy Warhol: From A to B and Back Again* (Boston: Houghton Mifflin, 2014), 62.

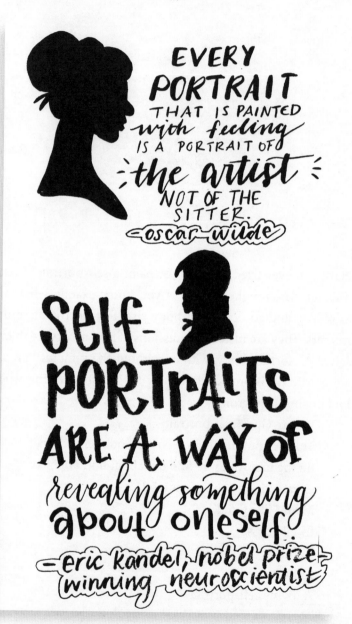

EVERY PORTRAIT THAT IS PAINTED with feeling IS A PORTRAIT OF the artist NOT OF THE SITTER.
—oscar wilde

SELF-PORTRAITS ARE A WAY OF revealing something about oneself.
—eric kandel, nobel prize winning neuroscientist

And one thing that this self-portrait reveals about the artist is that collaboration is at the very core of who God is. That's why words like *communion* and *community* are so important in God's vocabulary. God longs for togetherness because he is altogether collaborative himself.

Now, there is only one God.[25] Yet, as one smart British theologian puts it, the Bible frequently "speaks of three personal agents, Father, Son, and Holy Spirit, working together in the manner of a team."[26]

Another word for *team*? A *collab*. The ancient Hebrew word *Elohim*, that we translate into English as "God," is, grammatically speaking, plural. The *God collab*.[27] This isn't to be confused with polytheism or pantheism like in Greek mythology. There are not multiple gods competing with one another or operating out of any sort of insecurity. But we have to recognize the collaborative nature of God.

Take a look at what's happening in the first three verses of Genesis 1:

> In the beginning, *God*[28] created the heavens and the earth.
> And the *Spirit of God*[29] was hovering over the surface of the waters.
> Then God *said*,[30] "Let there be…"

---

25 If you want, you can dive into the Hebraic idea of God in passages like these: Deuteronomy 6:4–5; Isaiah 44:5–45:25.

26 Packer, *Concise Theology*, 40.

27 While *Elohim* is a plural form of a word, when used in reference to Israel's God, it is singular in its focus. This just highlights the "wholeness" of God… he is not lacking in any way. Any discussion of *Elohim* needs to remain grounded in the Hebraic understanding of God: one true God (*Elohim*; Deuteronomy 6, for example). The Trinity is Christianity's way of trying to explain this reality, evidenced throughout both the Old and New Testaments.

28 Referring to the Father.

29 Referring to the Holy Spirit.

30 Referring to Jesus, the Word of God.

This is the *God collab* at work. The creative outpouring of Father, Son, and Holy Spirit. The one true God, brilliantly creating in perfect unity and peace.

Theologians refer to this as the *Trinity*.[31]

Later, when the apostle John introduced Jesus in his eyewitness account, this is how he described Jesus: "In the beginning was the *Word*, and the *Word was with God*, and the *Word was God*."[32] In other words, Jesus is the Creator. He was "with" God…and he was God. The Word.

That's how a collaborative creative speaks.

Unfathomably incredible.

Beyond what we could ask or imagine.

Later, when Jesus instructed his followers that they should baptize in the "*name* of the Father and of the Son and of the Holy Spirit,"[33] he was highlighting this "One God in Three Beings" idea. The *God collab*.

Why is this so important to pause and ponder?

When God created humans in his image, he created humans with an inherent identity as collaborators. God designed us to work in community. Together. Humans are, at their very core, creative collaborators.

This is evident in the way Genesis says we were made. The teamwork of the *God collab* is made obvious, "Let *Us* make man in *Our* image, according to *Our* likeness."[34]

This creation event was the first and most epic collab ever!

The next verse says that "God created man in His own image."[35]

---

31 The cool girl from *The Matrix* isn't the only awesome Trinity there is.
32 John 1:1–3, NIV (emphasis added).
33 Matthew 28:19, NIV (emphasis added).
34 Genesis 1:26, NKJV (emphasis added).
35 Showing the oneness of the *God collab*.

Then, in case you missed it the first time, it repeats the point: "In the image of God He created them."

When something is repeated in the Bible, take notice. It's usually significant. In this case, the artist is instilling something remarkable in this final act of creation—himself.

We are God's fingerprint in this world. His mini-me.

The evidence of God's handiwork is everywhere. But in humans—God is stamped.

And if it wasn't enough that God made humankind in the *God collab*'s image, God took it a step further.

God breathed into the self-portrait.

Here's how the moment is described in the second chapter of Genesis: "Then the LORD formed the man from the dust of the ground. He breathed the breath of life into the man's nostrils, and the man became a living person."[36]

God.

Breathed.

Into.

Adam's nostrils.[37]

Adam came to life. His lungs expanded. He breathed out. He opened his eyes.

And he saw God.

Staring at him.

Smiling at him.

Saying, "Hello, Dirt-man! Come *imaginate* with me."

The cool thing about God is that he isn't an old stuffy Scrooge who got the world going with a bang and then just let it unfold. God didn't set the earth to spinning and then go out to run errands. No, God created a creature that he put his

---

36 Genesis 2:7, NLT.
37 Random…but did you know that if you put your mouth over someone's nose and blow, you can make them honk like a goose?

own breath into. God put his own life into "man" for the purpose of collaborating with him. Our souls, intelligence, ability to be creative, ability to discern and enjoy beauty, all hinge on this divine interaction. Filling our lungs with "breath" is God's beautiful way of expressing how he intentionally instilled the essence of his personhood within us. Just as parents pass on their genes and characteristics to their children, God created us in his likeness in order to pass his vision and talents on to us.

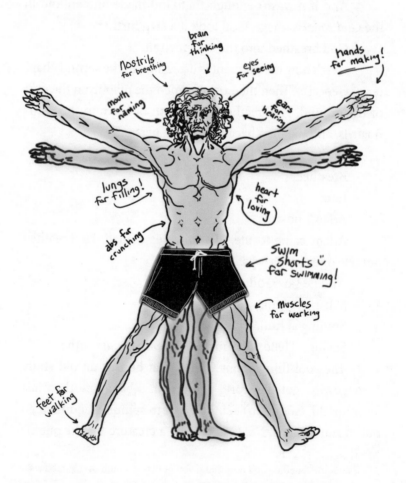

God didn't do that for any other created being.

God only did that for humankind. God chose humanity to be unique. God selected humanity to know his presence within them. God positioned humanity above the rest.

The Genesis word for "breath" in Hebrew is *ruach*. This is the same word for "spirit."

His *ruach*.

His Spirit.

His breath.

In us.

With us.

Through us.

We were created to have the breath of God alive within us. We were formed to be alive with his Spirit.

The poets of ancient Greece surmised, "We are his offspring."[38] Paul said, "For in him we live and move and have our being."[39] We are unique from the rest of the animal kingdom.

And so, though we are mere "creatures" of his creation, we are invited into his collaborative nature. We are indwelled with his breath. Made out of his collaborative desire to create artistic companions.

And, as stated earlier, not because God was lonely. God wasn't stuck in the mundane happenings of eternal boredom wishing he had someone to talk to, so out of some empty feeling of isolation, he created us to give him some company.

Not at all! Instead, the creation account shows that God was already whole in his collaborative community. Complete. Not lacking in any way. God already had companionship within himself. God was not needing anything or anyone else.

---

38 Acts 17:28, NIV.

39 Acts 17:28, NIV.

We were not created out of lack or need. Instead we were created because of a much better reason.

We were created out of *want*.

Me…you…every human on this earth…is wanted.

Out of love! Out of a collaborative artistic desire to create a masterpiece.

God's self-portrait.

The expression of the greatest artist. Made in the image of a collaborative God.

And because we are made in God's image, it means humans are endowed with a *high calling of responsibility*—a mind-boggling authority to join God as co-creators in the ongoing care of God's artwork.

Co-creators.

Do you know what God's first recorded words to humans were?

"Be fruitful and increase in number."[40]

In other words, "Create."

Make more.

But perhaps the biggest clue to the collaborative nature of God's creativity is a peculiar moment in the creation story. After all that God had made, after calling everything "good," after creating Adam, God found something wrong.

Something not good.

Something off.

Like an artist studying his work, convinced there is something lacking, God wants us to hear his observation. God wants us to know what upsets his creative work.

Adam was alone.

If God exists in community…

---

40   Genesis 1:28, NIV.

…and mankind is made in his likeness…

…then mankind should also exist in community.

It is as if after creating Adam, God stepped back and observed the portrait and said, "Wait!"

It is incomplete.

Not finished.

Not good…yet.[41]

Alone, Adam was not an accurate self-portrait of God.

So, God created someone for man to collab with. To laugh with. To create with. To enjoy life with:

> So God created mankind in his own image,
>   in the image of God he created them;
>   *male and female* he created them.[42]

Genesis chapter 2 goes on to describe the artistic process of making Eve. This story shows us very vividly that nothing is ever boring in God's art studio! Instead, each work is wildly creative and wonderfully strange.

Flesh from Adam's flesh.

Woman.

In God's image. Male and female he created them.

Co-laboring to be fruitful and multiply over the earth. Making beautiful things together.

Without each other, incomplete.

In communion, whole.

Wondrously productive.

Creatives. Artists.

Commissioned by God.

Crafted to be craftsmen.

---

41   Genesis 2:18.
42   Genesis 1:27, NIV (emphasis added).

Endowed with the collaborative, creative essence of God.
Working together with God to *imaginate*.
Because God is all about making beautiful things.

A DREAM REALIZED

I made the life-altering decision to be a magician at the age of six.

Six!

Makes sense. I was born to be on stage.[43] Whenever we'd pass a marquee on a theater lit up with lights, I'd wonder, *How do I get my name up there?* When I heard that the number one fear of the majority of people is to be in front of other people, it simply did not compute with my brain. If anything, I have the opposite fear. The fear that one day people might not let me get up in front of them.

At the age of four, I was invited by my dad—an accomplished magician himself—to join him on stage. At first, I would do simple quests, like bringing him a magic wand or some other prop, but after a while, I was performing my own tricks.[44]

I was given my own stage name.[45]

---

43 I saw how much attention all the doctors, nurses, and my family gave me for my performance of being born, so I've craved to be on center stage ever since.

44 My signature trick as a kid was a classic called "the zombie ball." Just thought you'd like to know.

45 I was "Scooter" the clown. Yes…a clown…*face palm*.

BEST MAGICIAN STAGE NAMES

* all of the following were not their REAL names!

① HOUDINI ⟶
* named in honor of the French illusionist, Jean-Eugène Robert Houdin

② cardini

③ [—DAVID— COPPERFIELD]

⑤ the amazing johnathan

⑥ THE PROFESSOR

⑦ RICKY JAY

⑧ indre kole

⑨ MARLO

⑩ BURT WONDERSTONE

⑪ TOMMY WONDER

50

And, just like that, by six years old, I was officially a magician.

I loved it!

But…

I quickly discovered a significant problem.

I didn't know how to shuffle cards.

All the images of great magicians depicted on TV, in books, and even on Mickey Mouse cartoons included cards flying from one hand to the other and wizard-like card riffling and shuffling skills.

In awe of my dad's amazing "bridge shuffle," I begged him to teach me. Though my hands were still kid-sized, he patiently taught me how to separate the cards half-and-half into each hand. He showed me how to slowly dribble them down from my thumbs. How to interlace them. How to change my hand position with my thumbs on top in order to create the right amount of tension to produce the beautiful shape of the bridge shuffle. I fell in love with the captivating sound of the cards falling onto each other when I executed the shuffle correctly.

I practiced for hours upon hours. First with one deck of cards. Then I combined two decks to shuffle 104 cards. Once I mastered that, I combined three decks to bridge shuffle 156 cards. I tried to shuffle four decks, for a total of 208 cards, but my young hands were still too small.

My dad had all kinds of decks around the house. There were poker, mini, jumbo, square, and even round-sized decks. I began to notice differences in card quality (e.g., The United States Playing Card Company cards held up much better than the other decks we got from non-card companies like KLM and American Airlines). And it didn't take me long to figure out which deck I thought was the best:

To be exact, "Bicycle 808 Rider Back" playing cards.

First printed in 1881 by Russell, Morgan & Company, it became the most famous deck of cards that had ever been printed. The ace of spades and the joker designed for this deck of cards are widely accepted today as the standard that all other playing cards are measured against. The unique "air cushioned" finish[46] makes it one of the easiest-to-handle decks of cards. And for quite a long stretch of my life, the Bicycle 808 Rider Back became the only deck I wanted to use for magic.

Then in the early 2000s, high-quality custom decks with original artwork became all the rage.[47] Because they looked so awesome, because they were so unique and personalized, I drooled about the idea of someday having my own specially designed deck of cards.

Then I discovered "cardistry."

And I drooled some more.

Twin brothers Dan and Dave Buck thought up a new genre of card juggling and performance art by combining "cards" with "artistry." They popularized "card flourishes,"

---

46 The air-cushioned finish is now the standard for quality decks of cards. There are several companies from which you can have cards printed, but there are only really three places in the world that manufacture quality, "air-cushioned" finish cards: The United States Playing Card Company in Cincinnati, Ohio, The Expert Playing Card Company in Taiwan, and Cartamundi in Belgium. Almost every deck of quality playing cards, no matter who designs and produces it, comes from one of these three factories.

47 I am not talking about the kitschy, junky-type cards you'd find at tourist traps. Look, if you just want a deck of cheap cards for an event like a wedding or corporate celebration, and you do not care about the quality, there are several printing companies that can make them for you. The problem is that most of these decks break down very quickly and are not good to do magic with.

involving new expert card moves such as cuts, displays, fans, patterns, springs, and sequences that they did with flashy movements to demonstrate skill and dexterity. The Buck twins released their three-volume VHS instructional series devoted to these cool cuts and shuffles and changed the magic and card world.[48]

HOW TO BECOME A [CARDIST] IN FIVE EASY STEPS

1. have little to no social life.
2. watch endless hours of other cardists on social media.
3. put in ten thousand hours of practice on each move.
4. develop carpal tunnel.
5. upload a successful attempt to social media platform of choice.

Almost overnight, the market for customized decks of playing cards was flooded. And so was my deck collection! My

---

48   In the magic world, for years there were only a couple types of flourishes a magician would do. They might spring the cards from one hand to the other or do a fancy cut. But for the most part, card flourishes were looked down upon because it highlights the hand skills being used. Magicians learned their card sleights from gambling cheats. When cheating at cards, you do not want to demonstrate any ability or any hint of skill that might tip off other players that it is not a fair game. Because of this, magicians always wanted to make their sleights and skills invisible. But when this new "cardistry" came along, instead of hiding the skill involved, the artistry of the skill became an important part of the main performance.

friends and family members kept giving me different decks all the time. I started swimming in piles of unique decks of cards…dreaming of creating my own design in the future.

At one point I met a group of cardists. These guys had backpacks full of dozens of decks. And not one of these cardists did magic. I was confused. They had an interest in these small pieces of paper called playing cards that I didn't know was possible. The way they dissected each different aspect of a deck was mesmerizing to me. These cardists treasured the uniqueness of their special decks—from the thickness of the paper, to the types of inks, to the artwork used, to the overall themes as a whole. They even had decks with essential oils infused in order to create a certain smell. One deck smelled like grapes, another had the scent of orange Fanta, and one even had a coffee aroma! Listening to these guys, you would have thought they were standing in an art museum analyzing famous works of art.

Then it hit me.

Decks of cards are art.

Art we get to touch…not just look at in an art gallery, but art we get to handle and play with.

Up until that moment, I had viewed cards as a means to an end. A game. A magic prop. A tool.

Don't believe me?

Go find a deck of cards. Come on…I'll wait.

Got them? Good. Now, look at them.

Consider the face cards. Who are the portraits of the king, queen, and jack cards modeled after? Are they actual royalty or possibly friends of the artist? Notice the unique fonts of the "pips" in the upper left and lower right corners of the cards that assign each card their number and suit identity.

Who decided that the king of hearts should have a dagger going into his head? Or why do the jack of hearts and jack of spades only have one eye, but the others have two? Is the design on the back of the cards elaborate or minimalistic?[49] All of these were artistic decisions.

The performance artist in me became absolutely convinced that I had to have my own custom deck. So, I dove in the deep end. I researched. I geeked out.[50] I asked questions. I uncovered layers and layers of information. I learned about paper stocks, ink types, "finishes," quality-controls, on and on.

Step 1: Choosing the Theme

The first step, I realized, in designing a customized deck was to select a theme. This needed to be personal…something that captured my uniqueness, my passions, my experiences, and my values. After brainstorming countless numbers of themes, I started a circular pattern around one that took me back to my roots—back to the environment that introduced me to my first decks of cards: travel.

During my elementary and junior high years, my family lived in different parts of Saudi Arabia. My dad, who performed his magic more as a hobby, worked for the oil company Saudi Aramco. Because of this, our family would fly around the world every year at least once—and this was well before

---

49 If this is piquing your interest, here are some other questions to ponder: How thick do the cards feel? What color is the back design? Is it a one-way back design, or is it mirrored so it looks the same no matter its orientation to the rest of the cards? What type of card stock is the card box (or tuck) made out of? Is there an overall theme to the cards? So many things to consider!

50 By the way…I wrote over three thousand words about all this that had to be cut. My publisher told me that "unless someone wants to make their own deck of cards, it's too much." But if that is you…write me and let's jam and geek out together!

each seat had its own TV screen or power outlet. I've got to tell you, this ADHD boy would get beyond bored on those twenty-seven-hour plus travel days. First, I'd use my Nintendo Game Boy for a couple of hours until the battery died. Then, I'd ask the attendants for the airline cards[51] and pass the hours annoying the person sitting next to me with shuffles and riffles and springs.

And finally I had landed on the theme of my very own custom deck. A travel mantra that journeyed with me wherever I went:

Make road life fun!

Step 2: Designing the Graphics

With the theme in place, next I found an incredible graphic artist, Carl Krokstedt, to work on the design. Carl and I drew our inspiration from the opening credits of the traveling-themed movie, *Catch Me If You Can*.

Step 3: Picking the Name

The deck also needed a name. With so many custom decks already out there, it was difficult to find a unique name that captured the travel theme.[52] But my buddy, Erik Casey, in a brilliant *imaginating* session, suggested "Planes, Trains & Automobiles." It was perfect. I love that old Steve Martin, John Candy, and John Hughes movie. And it also perfectly described the theme.[53]

---

51   This was back when airlines were luxury travel and every airline had its own deck of cards. Malaysian Airlines cards were my favorite airline deck.

52   My first desired name, "Travelers," had already been taken.

53   If you look at the card backs, you'll see planes, trains, and automobiles all over them.

Step 4: Ordering the Production

At first, the production application for The United States Playing Card Company overwhelmed me. I was stumped. There were so many options on the order form. I had no clue if I wanted my finish to be embossed or smooth. Did I want the cards punched face up or face down? I realized I had also forgotten to design a seal for the card box. I called an emergency phone meeting with different friends who had experience with the card-making process. Eventually, with their help and my fingers crossed, I submitted an order.

Step 5: Opening My Very Own Custom Deck

For four years, I had dreamed about being able to hold my own customized deck. So, I was beyond giddy on the day the cards finally arrived. From the gold foil on the card box, to the tangible feel of the smooth black paper I had selected, to the limited-edition numbered seal that was on each box, the deck simply looked and felt amazing.

I had all of this excitement, and I hadn't even broken the seal to play with the cards yet.

When I grew brave enough to open the box, the angels in the heavenly realms paused all they were doing to sing the "Hallelujah Chorus" as light shone down from on high. The cards levitated out of the box and into the air, on display for the whole world to ooh and ahh in wonder. Justin Bieber, Jimmy Fallon, and the pope all stopped by to bless this incredible event.

Or at least that's what happened in my mind. I can hardly begin to describe how excited I was as I first shuffled my very own custom deck of cards.

A dream accomplished.

A work of art in my hands.

That's How Collaborative Creativity Works

Why am I telling you about this dream realized?

You might be able to appreciate my passion for the subject, but at the same time you might think that I'm some sort of obsessive card fanatic flirting with a compulsive addiction. And you'd be right! *Ha!*

The love and passion I have for playing cards is ridiculous. I know that. And I love it! Opening a new deck of cards I haven't seen before is so exciting. Within ten to thirty seconds of opening up a deck, I can tell you way more about the cards than you would probably ever care to know. I geek out on the manufacturer's choice of paper stock, the inks they used, the sheen of the cards' finish, and even where in the world the deck was printed. I'm like a wine aficionado but with cards. I'm like a mountain climbing enthusiast but with decks instead of cliffs. I'm like a master gardener in spades and diamonds. All these details mean so much to me, and they fascinate me.

And my hope is that you'll get excited about it too. My desire is that, in some way, you'll appreciate cards a little bit more because you appreciate me and notice something that I care so much about.

PEOPLE LOVE WHAT OTHER PEOPLE ARE PASSIONATE ABOUT.

– LA LA LAND

Here's my point:

If this is how much passion I have for some pieces of paper that I got to help design and create, how much more does our Creator care about the things he designed and created?

God made the trees the card stock came from. God fashioned the pigments, resin, solvents, and other ingredients in the ink. He formed the ore for the metal that makes up the machines that manufactured the cards.

I wonder if we would humble ourselves enough to love what God gets passionate about?

God decided to *imaginate* everything in our universe… and we owe it to him (and ourselves) to pause and marvel.

There really is something to be said about actually stopping to smell the roses. Something significant happens when we take our eyes from a screen to look around at the world and get all nerdy about it.

Go ahead. Geek out about clouds, rocks, plants, and everything you can see. But don't stop there. Ponder the invisible things too.[54] Every day, find time to appreciate everything that God created and is so passionate about.

Everything.

God is more passionate about every part of his creation than you or I ever could be. As an artist, he remembers the exact process and decision that he put into creating everything. He remembers coming up with the theme, designing the graphics, coming up with names, ordering production, and opening it all up.

---

54   For example, the oxygen-carbon dioxide cycle. God is so creative that he embedded us into his ongoing collaborative creativity. He invented photosynthesis, a process by which green plants absorb carbon dioxide and convert it to oxygen. Because they do that, we can breathe. And when we breathe, we, in turn, expel carbon dioxide for the green plants to absorb and photosynthesize. This is the perfect cycle of life. That "simple" cycle is why you are alive.

And he remembers that after creating everything, he stepped back to exclaim:

It is good.

Here is some blank space
where you can geek out!
What parts of creation amaze you?

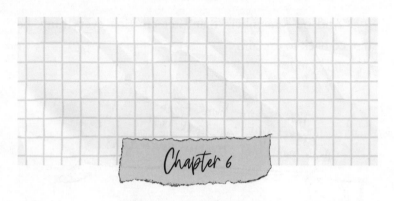

ART IS ESSENTIAL

ESSENTIAL

synonyms	antonyms
ABSOLUTELY NECESSARY	NONESSENTIAL
CRUCIAL	NEEDLESS
IMPERATIVE	TRIVIAL
INDISPENSABLE	UNIMPORTANT
INDISSOLUBLE	UNNECESSARY
REQUIRED FOR LIFE	OPTIONAL

During the pandemic year of 2020, the word *essential* took on a central role in our vocabulary. For a while across the country, only "essential" industries remained available: Grocery stores, gas stations, emergency rooms, and so on. But anything deemed "nonessential" was closed down. This included all live entertainment. In fact, any entertainment that encouraged people to gather together in crowds was shut down. My performing art, which had always been kind and friendly fun that helped droves of people smile and laugh, was suddenly considered dangerous. I understood why this happened, but still…Having my passion, my art, bear the label "nonessential" and "dangerous" was gut-wrenching. So, just like every other performing artist in 2020, I was forced to move to the flat dimensional world of virtual platforms.

Did someone say "Zoom fatigue"?

So depleting.

So defeating.

When sports no longer could have "fans in stands," when Broadway shows went "dark," when movie theaters had empty parking lots, and art museums closed their doors… people's souls were sapped dry.

In a few days, the world became so bleak.

Dark.

Bland.

Hopeless.

Nonessential.

I began to feel nonessential myself.

I will never forget the day my kiddos were finally able to go back to in-person school. There were so many new rules to keep everyone safe and to stop the spread of COVID-19. I was blown away by all the regulations but especially in my daughter's choir class. There could only be a certain number of students in each choir class: five. Five singers is not called a choir; it's a quintet. They had to stand apart at least six feet from each other. They had to wear both masks *and* face shields because when those students started singing, they were going to expel way too many germs, breath, and saliva. Honestly, part of me wondered if it was worth it. It seemed like too much trouble.

But then one day my daughter came home with her brand-new choir shirt. For this year, they decided to have the choir shirt say just three words. In big, bold letters it read:

Singing is essential.

Yes! Of course! It didn't matter how hard it was or how many hoops to jump through…singing is essential. Humans need to sing.

And laugh.

And express.

And act.

And celebrate.

And praise.

And hope.

And *imaginate* together.

Art is good for the heart. It is the flavor of this life.

There's an old bumper sticker I love that says:

Earth without "art" is just "Eh."

Because: *Art is essential.*

We need art to live…at least a life worth living.

Recently, I got to visit New York City with my wife and son to celebrate his tenth birthday. In our family, we intentionally identify and celebrate major milestones in our kids' lives. A tenth birthday is a big deal. So we decided that for their tenth birthdays, our kids get to travel with just Mom and Dad to New York City to see all the city has to offer.

Sadly, due to all the shutdowns of the pandemic, and Broadway being dark for eighteen months, my son's trip had to be delayed ten months. During those long months, he would ask over and over if we had planned his trip yet. We had to remind him repeatedly that until the world opened back up, we couldn't make any plans.

Finally, when it was deemed safe to travel again, we were all bursting with excitement as we boarded the plane destined for the Big Apple. My son's excitement for everything from the Nintendo flagship store to the Harry Potter store to how tall the buildings were was infectious. We explored, laughed, and made all the memories.

New York is huge. But the world is small. While exploring the city, we just happened to run into one of my magician friends on the streets. He told us he was so excited because he had somehow scored tickets to that night's performance of the Broadway show *Aladdin*. I wanted to share in his excitement but didn't fully grasp why he was excited until he explained that it was the re-opening night for the show.

Re-opening night!

After eighteen months of Broadway being dark.

For kicks, I checked to see if there were any tickets left... and to my shock and surprise, there were three tickets...in the second row...for a third of the normal price. I have no idea why they were still available or why they were so cheap (maybe the theater slashed the prices because it was so close to showtime?), but we immediately bought the tickets.

When we arrived at the theater, the energy was electric. Each person in attendance was part of the history of a beloved Broadway show getting to open its doors again—not for a digital Zoom performance but for an actual, live, in-person audience.

There was a camera crew live-streaming the opening on TikTok. The original composer of the Broadway musical, Alan Menken, was in attendance. Broadway legend Kristin Chenowith was six rows behind us with her entourage. And there we were in the second row on this epic night!

Yes, Tony-winner Kristin had to stare at the red mop of my head. Beyond crazy!

When the house lights went down and the orchestra started its overture, you could feel the entire theater's excitement. "Broadway is back!" At the end of the number "Friend Like Me," the cast had to pause for a good five minutes as every person in attendance jumped to their feet giving one of the biggest standing ovations I have ever experienced.

Though the actors on stage were trying to hold and stay in character, you could see them one by one start to break in little ways, fighting back smiles and tears of joy as we continued to cheer. Every break for applause was quadrupled. At the final curtain call, the whole place went into pandemonium.

The actors and musicians played their hearts out. But after a while, we were no longer just cheering because it was an incredible performance. We were also cheering that we were able once again to gather together and experience art in a public place. We applauded that Broadway was not dead. We applauded because *art is essential!*

God believes this so much that he not only creates art himself, but he also divinely inspires it.

Equipped for Artistry

God never intended art to be useless or frivolous. God intended art to be central to his creation and vital to our collaboration with him.

There was a time when God pulled Moses aside on Mount Sinai to *imaginate*. The Israelites were in the desert after having escaped from Egypt. God wanted to establish the laws and customs for this wandering nation. A major part of this vision included building the first house of worship, the tabernacle—the place where God promised to dwell.

Now, just like if you were the one meeting with an architect and builder to design and construct your home, this was a really big deal to God. God wanted his home to be perfect. God didn't want any low-quality materials to be used. He didn't want the builders to cut any corners or hurry the job with any boring pre-fab pieces.

But he didn't want to do all the work himself either. As is his usual style, he wanted to accomplish his plan through a collab with humans.

THE TRUE WORK OF ART IS BUT a SHADOW OF THE divine perfection

– michelangelo

So it is deeply significant that we are told the following:

Then the LORD said to Moses, "See, I have chosen *Bezalel*…and I have *filled him with the Spirit of God*, with wisdom, with understanding, with knowledge and with all kinds of skills—*to make artistic designs* for work in gold, silver and bronze, to cut and set stones, to work in wood, and to engage in all kinds of crafts. Moreover, I have appointed *Oholiab* son of Ahisamak, of the tribe of Dan, to help him. Also I have *given ability* to all the skilled workers to make everything I have commanded you.[55]

I've heard that to get your name in the Bible, you either had to give birth to somebody's ancestor, do something really stupid, or be in collaboration with God.

These two guys with crazy names—Bezalel and Oholiab[56]—were in collaboration with the Divine.

God chose them to create something for him.

God contracted and commissioned them to create a work of art.

And not just any art. To create his tabernacle.

His dwelling place.

The home of God on earth.

I'd say that sounds rather essential.

A place for God to live…with us.

God with us.

Because he wants to collab.

Creatively.

"Filled with the Spirit of God…to make artistic designs…"

What? How incredible is that!

God says art is divine.

Art is supernatural.

Art is inspired.

Art comes from God.

Art is an expression of God.

---

55 Exodus 31:1–6, NIV (emphasis added).

56 If you've ever heard me speak in person on this subject, you know I always have a hard time pronouncing their names.

So, artistry and skills are given to us.

By God.

God literally says he has given divine, supernatural inspiration to make art.

Because creating, expressing, participating in, and enjoying all the different forms of art is essential to how God created us and everything in this world.

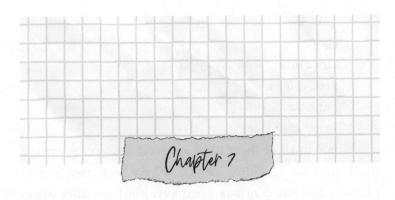

FINDING CREATIVITY

The most fun yet most difficult part of my job as a magician is finding new ideas. As wise King Solomon wrote millennia ago, "There is nothing new under the sun."[57] Yet, when I'm invited back to perform for people over and over, they want and expect new magic tricks.[58] Also, the creative in me would never want to stay stagnant. So I will often ask my friends (and even sometimes complete strangers) random questions to try to spark a new concept for a trick.

Eight years ago, I attended a magic conference in Cheltenham, England. Side note...yes there are magic conventions. Yes, they are amazing. Yes, they also can be weirder than a comic con. Visualize hundreds of geeky magicians gathering to talk for literally hours about sleight of hand, cards, coins, cubes, and secret moves.

I often use this breeding ground of creativity to try to come up with my next ideas.

Here's the question I asked everyone that weekend:

"If you had actual 'God-like powers,' what would you do?"

---

57   Ecclesiastes 1:9, ESV.
58   I often envy musicians who are invited back to play their "greatest hits."

I got a lot of the same answers:

"Fly."

"Move things with my mind."

"Read minds."

"Time travel."

"Shape-shift things."

Though all of these ideas are great concepts for magic tricks, they are also ideas magicians have been playing with for years and will continue to explore. But I was after something brand new. Something unique…something fresh.

Then one of the fellow conference attendees, Sharky,[59] said this:

"Total God-like powers? I'd create a new color."

Boom.

My mind melted.

Such a killer idea! I had been thinking inside the box of what has already been created, and he spoke to something altogether new. Something that is impossible without God-like powers. An addition to creation. A new color on the color spectrum and new light on the light spectrum. A shade that no one has ever seen or had a chance to name.

This idea has sat with me since then and inspired me to always think outside the box…or even try to imagine there is no box at all. To try to have "God-like" thoughts, and not just in creating a magic trick, but also in life.

To not just think in my current world view.

To dream outside of what I know.

God created us in his image, as his self-portrait.

We were created to act and think like him.

---

59 Sharky is one of the greatest magic consultants in all the world and has consulted for every major magician in Europe…and yet he's not a magician himself!

We were asked to *imagine*.

But for some insane reason, we decided to ignore his ways and got stuck thinking within a narrow box of ideas. In a sense, we acted like bratty toddlers who ignored the protective warnings not to touch the red-hot stove top. In essence, we thought our small reasoning skills were better than God's.

Before we decided to ignore his ways, I am sure we acted and thought like God.

My youngest son, Jude Sinatra, is my mini-me. His older brother, Silas John-Paul, takes after my wife's side of the family. His older sister, Charity Joy, shares my hair color and personality, but as a girl, she's not as close of a replica. Jude Sinatra looks like me, has a joy and passion for life like me, and often wants to do whatever Daddy is doing.

If I'm cooking, he wants to cook in his play kitchen. If I'm wearing my San Francisco Giants hat, he wants to wear his San Francisco Giants hat. He thinks, "If Daddy can do it, why can't Jude Sinatra also do it?" He loves to walk next to me and is my little dude.

Before we stiff-armed God, we walked with him in the garden. We acted like him and even created like him. Can you picture this in your mind? Can you see Adam following God around, asking too many questions like every toddler does, trying to discover everything about this new world? What's that? What's a tree? What is growing on the tree? What's a fruit? Why can't I eat that fruit? Can you envision God almost tripping over Adam sometimes because Adam was following so close?

God breathed into Adam's nostrils and then placed his mini-me in a garden. And not just any garden: *the* garden.

Eden.

God designed Eden with the perfect irrigation of four rivers: Pishon, Gihon, Tigris, and Euphrates. Then God put his new little talkative shadow in charge of taking care of that garden. God must have explained how plants grow, how to trim saplings, pick fruit, tend to the soil. Adam must have stopped over and over to eat an orange or climb a banyan tree or, literally, smell the roses.[60]

Then, I imagine God looked at his man cub and smiled.

I picture a scene where God sat Adam down on a rock, handed him a cup of fresh lemonade and some fig newtons, and prepared him for the coolest zoo-on-parade ever.

One by one, or perhaps two by two, the animals paraded before Adam, with God joyfully conducting the event. As the first animal presented itself to Adam, God said: "Adam, I want you to name this animal."

"*Me?*"

"Yes, you."

"But you made this animal."

"And I want you to join me in the creative process."

"Uh…okay…This one will be called a…"

Can you imagine how creatively exhausting it would be generating a new name for every animal on earth? At first you might be a little bit creative. But how long do you think you could endure?

Lion.

Cheetah.

Jaguar.

Cougar.

---

60 Can you imagine being the first human to smell a flower? Was their fragrance even better before the world got screwed up? I'm so thankful that God left us the traces and scents of his good artwork so that we could find our trail back to him.

Leopard.

Um...that one is white like snow, but it looks just like a leopard...um...*snow* leopard?

Peacock.

Crow.

Dove.

Sparrow.

Goose.

Ostrich.

Pigeon.

Turkey.

Chicken.

Cardinal.

Um...okay another bird...and it's blue...um...bluebird?

Anteater...because it eats what looks like ants...oh, wait...those are termites. Too late. I thought they were ants, and I have too many others to get through today. Sorry, bud, you're an anteater.

Next?

Orca.

Humpback whale.

Yikes! Killer whale!

Blue whale.

Uh...gray whale?[61]

---

61   Let's recognize that I'm just having fun imagining this. Of course, Adam didn't even speak English, so who knows what names he actually gave each animal in his "Eden-ese" language. But think about how crazy of a job that must have been.

The only way Adam could have continued to be creative enough to accomplish such a task was to reach down deep into who he was created to be. God created Adam with the attributes of the most Creative Being in the universe. And God created Adam to be inspired and equipped by God's Spirit in the creative process.

What We Were Designed to Do

Here's what I'm getting at: We all have the ability to be that creative.

I'm talking to my artsy people:

Many of you are like me. You love art in all its forms; visual art, performing art, you love it all. You might even refer to yourself as a creative. Maybe that's why you were interested in this book in the first place.

And to my non-artsy people:

Some of you, even if you have an appreciation for art, do not consider yourself to be creative. Often my math friends or sports buddies fall into this category. And I would give you the same push that I would give the artsy folks: you are also given creative abilities. It might not be the ability to draw or sing. But think about the things you're good at. I'm sure no matter what it is, it takes some form of a creative process to accomplish. For example, I have a dentist friend who doesn't think he is very creative. Yet, every day he rebuilds teeth and produces healthy, beautiful smiles. It pains me (literally) to say it, but my friend uses an artistic touch when he is cleaning and filling and bracing and bridging and drilling.[62] If he drills too deep, it will expose the nerve, causing all sorts of new problems. If he drills too shallow, the problem will not be fixed. Even the way he injects Novocain to numb my gums is creative. What he sees

---

62 Sorry if this made you cringe.

simply as work involves so much constant creativity and collaboration and problem solving that it baffles my mind. And in the end, he produces something good out of the mess of my mouth. He serves as an example of how any of us, with any *honed craft*, can use our skills to create.

If you have made it this far in the book, I hope I have at least convinced you that you were created by an artist, in his image with his attributes. Though we all go about life in different ways, we all do it creatively.

In high school, there is this lie that there are fine arts people and then there are jocks. As if jocks can't be creative and choir and band nerds can't be good at sports. Though I am the biggest theater nerd, I am also a huge baseball fan. In fact, I love baseball so much that one favorite team isn't quite enough for me. That's right, I root for two different teams, one on each coast and each league. My National League team is the San Francisco Giants. My American League team is the New York Yankees.[63] During baseball season, I keep up with both teams, all 162 games per team. During the spring, summer, and fall, there are a lot of baseball games on our TV.

One of the things I love to watch is a batter's hitting stance. Some stand straight up and down. Some turn their front foot inward so much I cannot imagine it being comfortable. Some hunch over all scrunched up into a ball. Some crowd the plate, menacing and unafraid. And some, like one of my favorite Giants players, Hunter Pence, seem to bounce in the box like Tigger.

---

63 If you are also a baseball fan, yes, I recognize the oxymoronic nature of rooting for those two teams. It's a long story. If you want to hear it, write me on socials.

Now, when I was on the local third grade Little League team, my coach taught us the "proper hitting stance." I have never seen one of these big league players use the "proper hitting stance." I'm not saying that my Little League coach was lying to us. I think we all must start with the fundamentals before branching out. But then we must find our own unique style.

Whether you are an artist working on an oil painting, a big leaguer getting ready to hit a baseball, an architect designing a building, a singer practicing a song, or even a dentist filling a cavity, all our pursuits require us to be creative.

And when we are creative, we get to be like God, our Creator.

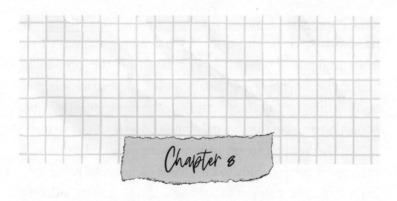

PAINTING OVER ALL THE WALLS

How old are you?

Let me date you or me with this question: Do you remember when Taylor Swift sang country?

I so wish there was a real-time social media poll in this book to know how all of you answered!

While I was driving my twelve-year-old daughter to school one day, I happened to be playing an Apple playlist of random music. An old Taylor Swift song started playing...like an *old* Taylor Swift song. Well, Taylor was young back then. Which means the song is old. Old. Like from her first album released in 2006. Ancient. Back when pterodactyls were flying around.

My daughter was instantly confused. "How is this Taylor Swift? It's country."

I think I must have snort laughed or something. Have you ever done that? And I just had to smile and shake it off.[64] I remember how crazy everyone got when Taylor transitioned

---

64 Yes, I meant to make the "Shake It Off" reference.

from poppy-country to pure pop. I explained to my daughter that true creatives often go through different stages.[65]

Take Pablo Picasso's "Blue Period."[66] After learning of his friend's suicide, Picasso withdrew into a major depression, and for three years, he painted almost solely in blue and green tones. At the time, no one appreciated his blue works. He had started to gain some popularity in the hip art town of Paris, and the populous didn't want him to change. Yet creatives often need to do new things, and so they do.

The All-In Creative Process

My wife loves interior design. Not only is she an incredible designer herself, but she also loves to observe and appreciate the designs of others. She is constantly introducing me to new interior designs in shows, magazines, and on social media. Because I like to be around her, I now know the names of Chip and Joanna Gaines, other HGTV home reno stars, and many an Instagram DYI-er.

There is one designer/muralist my wife loves named Racheal Jackson. This woman's creativity amazes me! Jackson's ability to paint bold-colored curvy stripes is simply inspiring. Yes, you read that right, someone painting curving stripes inspires me. If you think I'm weird, just put a bookmark on this page and check out her stuff online.

---

65   There's an old Billy Crystal joke that goes along similar lines. He tells the story of when his daughter came to him one day quite confused. When he asked what was going on, she responded, "Dad, was Paul McCartney in a group before Wings?" (Sorry, if you are too young to get this one. Please, please, please Google it.)

66   You mean he had a stage before "Cubism"? Uh, yeah. And a whole bunch of other "periods" of work too: the Blue Period, the Rose Period, the African Period, Cubism, Neoclassicism, Surrealism, and more. I'm telling you, creatives go through different stages!

Jackson uses the brightest colors. When I first started to follow her work, I would often doubt her vision. "That is way too bold," I'd think. "There's no way all those bright colors will work together." Yet again and again, I would be amazed at how she could pull off such fearless designs.

Though she often travels to paint commissioned murals for others, her main canvas is in her own home. She has a massive social media following that tunes in daily to see what big bold new thing she is painting in her bathroom, laundry room, living room, basement. Basically, any place in her house that hasn't been retouched recently is a potential canvas. I have watched her renovate and paint almost every corner of her house to the point where I feel like I could visit her and feel at home. (Maybe that's slightly creepy?)

One time she announced something on her socials that shocked me (and most of her followers). On a whim, Jackson and her husband decided to buy a house and move. The first reaction many of her followers had was, "What will you do with all those bold murals in your house?" She heard the worries and answered very simply, "We're going to paint over all the walls."

What! The results of all the hours spent creating and painting would now be covered in boring, move-in primer and paint? Racheal made this decision for several reasons, including to protect her work. She decided they needed to turn their house back into a blank palette for the next residents. Her home had merely been a rental. They had just borrowed that space for a while.

Mind blown.

What Jackson and her husband did is everything opposite of what my human nature wants to do.

And so, my wife and I tested this idea. (Not on purpose.)

My wife, Maribeth, decided we should reno our boring back yard. We sat down to *imaginate* what it could look like. She Pinterested a bunch of incredible ideas, and we finally landed on one. It would be an extended, modern-style patio with big pavers and small rocks in between, creating a cool, grid-type pattern. We dug out the grass for the new patio and set the pavers, but then we could not find the right color of rock that my wife had envisioned in her decoratively gifted imagination.

We researched on the internet and visited several rock supply places looking for what we wanted. Finally we found something that we thought would work. We borrowed my dad's truck to pick up the rock. After a forty-five-minute drive, and passing at least four other rock suppliers, we arrived at our chosen landscaping store. But when we arrived, the rock, which we thought would be perfect, looked slightly different then how it had appeared on the webpage. Feeling stuck after driving that whole way, we did not want to leave empty handed. So we bought the "okay" looking rocks and drove home. Several sweaty hours later, we had unloaded and painstakingly placed every single rock between the pavers.

Then we stepped back to admire what we had accomplished. We took turns trying to put a positive spin on all our hard work. We torqued our faces and tried different points of view, but the honest truth was...

Blah.

Not bad.

But not great.

It definitely wasn't what we had imagined or hoped for after all those hours of work. But we had gone to so much trouble, and it was ludicrous to think of changing plans at this point. So we went to bed hoping it would look better in the morning.

It didn't.

But it would be stupid crazy to try to dig up all those small rocks to replace them, right? Too much work had gone into it already. Too much effort to redo this project.

So we let it sit.

But after a week of trying to convince ourselves that we could live with it, we went shopping again, and we found rocks that finally matched our vision.

First, we got down on our hands and knees and picked up those blah rocks with small shovels and our hands, piece by piece, eventually clearing every one out of there.

Next, with giddy excitement, we picked up the new rocks that matched our vision. We unloaded and placed all the new rocks and breathed a deep sense of relief and joy. The final look of the project reminded us of our very own life-sized Zen garden with rake and all. It was worth the extra work to dig up the old and replace it with the new.

Remember, herein lies one of the most beautiful things about our Creator: he has not finished creating. (We touched on this back in chapter 3, but let's dive deeper.)

Many think God finished creating in Genesis. They see God as some kind of giant cosmic spark plug. That God just turned the key in the ignition to our world.

But after God "rested" on the seventh day, he got right back to work.[67] He engaged in a restoration effort to clean up Adam and Eve's vandalism. He painted a massive spectrum of colors in the sky after the flood. He collaborated with Moses to perform jaw-dropping wonders. He inspired David to write poetry and songs accompanied by musical scores. He stirred vivid pictures of his glory among the prophets. Every miracle Jesus performed was an indication that the Creator was still at work in his creation. And he is actively involved in the creative process to this day.

The more I do life with my Creator, the more I see him recreating me and this world daily. In Paul's second letter to the church in Corinth, he tells us: "Therefore, if anyone is in Christ, he is a new creation. The old has passed away; behold, the new has come."[68]

Our Creator is ready to grab a brush to join us in painting over the walls and getting down on his hands and knees to

---

67 I have a friend whose son, as a kid, thought that "God created the world in six days, and on the seventh day he got arrested."

68 2 Corinthians 5:17, ESV.

help dig up all the blah-looking rock of old. Those parts of our life that we have repetitively messed up. Those habits that we promised ourselves we wouldn't return to again. Addictions we cannot shake. Things we used to fill the void but that only ended up making us emptier. The walls we've put up to block our Creator.

God wants to start over with us by giving us a new portrait, made possible by Jesus.

A beautiful new creation.

His mercies in our life are new every morning.[69]

He will remake our heart of stone into a heart of love and joy.[70]

We will be born all over again into a new life.[71]

So here's the question: Are you willing to let God dig up the "old"? Are you willing for God to recreate you and dig up the bad rocks in your life? The problem with all this, of course, is patience. Mostly, our lack of it. It would be easier for us to answer "Yes" if it could happen instantly and if it didn't take determined effort. But that doesn't seem to be the case.

Surprised by Art

Maybe this will help.

Every time I get to see a famous piece of art in person, a piece that I have only seen in books, I get a little nervous. That might sound weird, but it's because I'm scared the art pieces won't live up to the hype. This is most true for me of the *Mona Lisa*. Though she is a beautiful painting and has earned all the praises of being one of Leonardo da Vinci's masterpieces, she is also kind of *under*whelming.

---

69   Lamentations 3:23.
70   Ezekiel 36:26.
71   John 3:16.

How she is displayed at the Louvre art museum in Paris has something to do with it. She is the only painting on the wall and is not that big nor that vibrant of a painting. Directly across from the *Mona Lisa*, though, is a ginormous painting entitled *The Wedding Feast at Cana*. Painted in lively colors with oils, the work by artist Paolo Veronese depicts Jesus' first miracle of turning water into wine. That painting fills the entire, giant wall.[72] The *Mona Lisa*, which is the size of a normal portrait,[73] seems dwarfed in its subtle brown tones. When you walk into the room with the *Mona Lisa*, it is confusing why everyone crowds around this small, dull painting, protected behind the most advanced security system in the world, when on the opposite wall is that dramatic mammoth of wedded wonder.

Recently, my wife and I got to experience the Metropolitan Museum of Art (called "The Met") in New York City. It did not disappoint.[74] I was most interested in seeing Van Gogh's *Self-Portrait with a Straw Hat* (which my middle son, Silas, once mistakenly thought was a painting of me) and Monet's *Bouquet of Sunflowers* (which always just makes me smile). To be able to stand in front of these paintings and gaze upon a master painter's work was a mesmerizing experience.

But another painting surprised me.

Now the first time I was surprised by a painting was when I was eighteen. I was visiting the State Hermitage Museum in St. Petersburg, Russia, with some friends. (Did I mention I've traveled around a bit?) Well, after spending three hours walking around the museum, I had seen so much art

---

72   *The Wedding Feast at Cana* painting is 22 ft. 3 in. x 32 ft.—crazy big!

73   The *Mona Lisa* painting's size is 2 ft. 6 in. x 1 ft. 9 in.

74   If you have not been to The Met, you owe it to yourself to go explore and be inspired.

that I had developed art-fatigue. Even if everyone else was still *oohing* and *ahhing* over a master painter's work, I was becoming more interested in how good lunch would look on my plate. But my friends wanted to see a few more things, so I followed them around with a bit of a growing headache and diminishing expectations. That's when I turned a corner and saw a huge crowd around a painting that raised goose-bumps instantly all over my body. The painting in front of my eyes took me by complete surprise. It was *The Return of the Prodigal Son* by Rembrandt. At the time, I had never heard of this painting, but it has since become one of my favorites. Rembrandt's use of dark and light and red shades captivated me like a tractor-beam.

Now, fast-forward with me back to our time at The Met. With Rembrandt's *Prodigal* painting in my mind, I was wondering what would surprise me this time. Though there were a lot of incredible pieces, in every medium of art possible, one piece stood out and drew me in. It was called *The Gardener* by Georges Seurat. Admittedly, when it comes to visual art, I am fairly ignorant. I love it, but my art history knowledge makes me a novice at best. When we came across *The Gardener*, I recognized the artist's name, but my wife had to educate me about his impact on the art world.

Georges Seurat is most famous for inventing the art form of pointillism—the practice of applying tiny dots of color to a surface so that when viewed from a distance, they visually blend together. Seurat's theory is that by separating the colors into little dots, it forces our eyes to do the blending of the colors and therefore causes more vibrancy of color in our minds. One of his most famous works in this method is *A Sunday on La Grande Jatte*. There are multiple books, art studies, and even a Pulitzer Prize-winning Broadway musical devoted to the study of this painting and the breakthrough that it made in the art world. It was painted with oils from 1884 to 1886, executed on a large canvas, and launched the Neo-impressionist art movement. Impressive!

Because of this, Seurat's earlier painting, *The Gardener,* hit me even more deeply. While *A Sunday on La Grande Jatte* is much grander and considerably more important in that it ushered in a revolutionary new art form, spawning new artistic eras, *The Gardener* grabbed my full attention because if you look at how Seurat painted it, you can see how he is in process. *The Gardener* was painted with oils from 1882 to 1883 on a small, humble wood plank. Seurat hadn't gotten to the point of pointillism yet, but you can see that he's striving to have a breakthrough. He is even using the same idea of applying colors with different brush strokes and letting the eye do the mixing, but in this painting, he is not quite bold enough yet— or mature enough yet—to just use dots.

He wouldn't make this breakthrough for another two years, but you can see the journey and the desire is there in *The Gardener*.

When I look at my own performing art of magic through the years, I can see this same sort of struggle and desire to strive forward. I have definitely not arrived at my *A Sunday on La Grande Jatte* by any extreme, and honestly do not know if I ever will in the field of magic. But this struggle, this desire, this journey...

This is also how I feel about my relationship with the Creator. Though my salvation is complete, though I have been forgiven, though "the old is gone and the new is here," though I am a "new creation" in Christ,[75] I still am very much in process.[76]

Already.

But not yet.

---

75 2 Corinthians 5:17, NIV.
76 See Philippians 2:12, discussing that we need to work out our salvation with fear and trembling.

Just like Seurat knew to push his art further, I know I need to push my relationship with God further.

When someone decides to become a follower of Jesus, there is a hope that he or she will just suddenly arrive, that everything will just be happily ever after. Like a girl who dreams and plans her wedding from the age of six. She has studied bridal magazines for so many years. But the end of the wedding ceremony is actually just the beginning of the marriage. When we first decide to entrust ourselves to God, we are fully saved. We are fully forgiven. We have full access to his Spirit. We are made new. And yet, we are also just at the beginning of our eternal relationship. If we stop there, we will miss God's best for us.

The wonder of discovering and aligning ourselves with the surprising creativity of God is part of the process.

We must keep trying to *imaginate* with him.

You are a living work of art.

You are not static.

You are being made new.

In Christ, you are saved.

But he is also not finished with you yet.

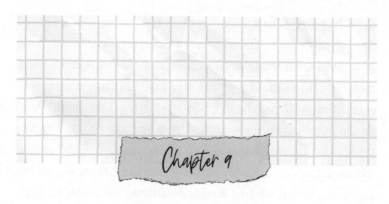

ART IS NOT SAFE

Here's my "I was bit by a lion in Africa and lived to tell about it" story:

My wife and I were invited to perform at a conference in South Africa. On our last night there, with the continual drive to #MakeRoadLifeFun, I asked one of my new local friends a question that now lives in infamy:

"So…is there any way I could see a lion before we leave?"

His fateful answer: "Heck yes, friend! Let's find you a lion!"

The next day my wife and I couldn't wait. We awoke early, excited to see lions in Africa. We didn't have time to go on a full-fledged safari because our flight left later that afternoon, but our new friends drove us to a local lion preserve. At this park, people could drive through different protected areas where the lions roam right outside the car. Multiple signs were posted everywhere that instructed drivers and their passengers to *"Keep your doors locked!"* I joked, "Like the lions can open your doors, heh heh." My friend gave me a look like, "You ignorant American," and then said, "Um…yeah, they can open your door. And there are lots of deaths every year because people don't obey the signs. And people think *the lions* are stupid."

I quickly realized we weren't at Disney World's Animal Kingdom.

Now, at this particular lion park, they had something called the "Lion Cub Experience." Visions danced in my head of all the surrounding animals singing "The Circle of Life" while I, like Rafiki, held up Simba the lion cub. And against both my wife's and South African friends' wise cautions, I signed us all up for the experience.

We waited outside the big, fifteen-foot-high gates to the enclosure where we'd get to play with these cute, little lion kittens. The fact that the gates were big enough to guard us from velociraptors didn't faze me. I was giddy with *Lion King* dreams.

The park's photographer/lion-handler came to let us into the "experience zone." As he unlocked the giant gates, I noticed that half of his uniform shirt was in shreds.

Not like a few worn-out cuts or frayed edges.

Shreds.

This should have been another warning…but my dumb, American, movie-mind didn't register a shredded shirt as danger. *Nope*, I thought to myself, *he must have gotten that either while doing his laundry, or maybe from his backyard chickens, or even perhaps while fending off the fictional experimental Jurassic dinosaurs that had escaped from the nearby lab. You know…because how else could his shirt have gotten ripped up so badly?*

Right before he swung open the gates, the handler gave us very strict warnings not to touch the cubs' heads or to turn our back on them. Well, that instruction went in one ear and quickly leaked out somewhere else.

As the gates slowly opened, we all got a peek at two cute cubs and expressed a series of uncontrollable utterances that progressed something like this: "Aw…what adorab… ummm…uhhhh…ohhhh my…woah there…"

These were no longer sweet little cubs. In the span of seconds, they went from what we thought were going to be cuddly little Simbas to two-hundred-fifty to three-hundred-pound lionesses. At six months to eight months old, they could eat me. And then they could still have room to consume Maribeth and our friends and our guide for dessert. On all fours, their noses came up to my stomach, and on their hind legs, they easily rose to over six feet tall.

But…we paid our money. And if it wasn't safe, they wouldn't let us be with them. Right?

At the encouragement of the handler, we started playing with the adorable man-eaters. For a bit, we played tug-of-war with a giant stick. Of course, due to their raw power, they always won (think, "Let the Wookie win."). We were able to pet them and take pictures with them.

At one point, while posing for a picture, I was on my haunches bent down petting one of them on the head. Yes, I know what the guy said, but he was petting her there, and it seemed to be working out fine for his shirt. So, I went for it. I just started nuzzling the noggin of one of the cubs.

And then…

Out of my peripheral vision, I saw the second one creeping slowly toward me, closing in on my jugular vein. In a scene reminiscent of the *Lion King*, I imagined this cub looked like Scar attacking an antelope. Realizing that I played the part of the antelope, I stood up quickly, but I instantly felt the cub's baseball mitts of paws pressed against my back, one on each shoulder blade.

As if the weight of her body wasn't enough on my back…

I felt her
lean down
and
bite
my love handle.

I wish I could tell you that in that moment I grabbed her and did some incredible king of the beast judo move to throw her off me.

I wish I could tell you I let out some manly war cry in front of my wife and new South African friends as I Tarzan-ed my way to freedom.

But…frightened six-year-old little girls have not hit the high screechy notes I hit when I screamed out in utter fear of being eaten alive in Africa.

The simple fact is that she was not trying to eat me or kill me. If she wanted to do either, she would have. And I would no longer be here to tell you this story.

She was still just a kitten. A very large, three-hundred-pound kitten. But still a kitten. Yes, a kitten capable of ripping out my intestines. But still a kitten. And like all kittens, she was playing and gave me a little love nibble.

Unfortunately, my tender suburban skin doesn't know the difference between a kitten playfully nibbling and a lion gnawing on a gazelle. So, my skin caved under the pressure of her powerful jaws and teeth, and I starting bleeding and bruising.

Thinking back on that moment, a normal reaction to being bitten by a wild animal bigger than oneself would have been to leave the experience immediately and seek medical attention. Even if I was not going to bleed out, wild animals carry different bacteria than humans.[77] Something in my survival instincts should have alarmed me enough to get out of there. At the least, I should have given more thought to the upcoming TSA questions about whether I had visited any petting farms while out of the country. (Why yes, in fact, yes, I did, dear travel security agent. Don't you see this open, oozing wound on my love handle?)

But the split second after being in the jaws of a lioness, when my performer's brain realized I was not going to die, I actually became so excited that one day I would get to tell this story about the time I traveled all the way to Africa and was bitten by a lion and lived to tell about it that I shut off all worry of offering myself up for dinner to six hundred pounds of cats and stayed and played with the two lions for another fifteen minutes.

---

77 This was also what my mother tried to insist on me doing...and my wife and the flight attendant to whom I told the story on the way home.

"ASLAN IS A LION—THE LION, THE GREAT LION."
"OOH!" SAID SUSAN.
"I'D THOUGHT HE WAS A MAN. IS HE—QUITE SAFE?
I SHALL FEEL RATHER NERVOUS ABOUT MEETING A LION."
..."SAFE?" SAID MR. BEAVER...
"WHO SAID ANYTHING ABOUT SAFE?
'COURSE HE ISN'T SAFE.
BUT HE'S GOOD."

- C. S. LEWIS, THE LION, THE WITCH AND THE WARDROBE

Why am I telling you this crazy story besides the point that I simply love to tell it with as much theatrics as I can as often as I can? To transition into the idea that creativity and art (visual, performance, or even how we creatively relate to this world) are not safe.

You can make safe "pop-art." You can perform a trick that you bought at the magic shop. Sing a song with friends at karaoke. You can paint walls in a house simply because they need some color without it getting scary.

But true art and creativity demand something that most of us are scared of: vulnerability.

To make art that is worth something, you must be willing to take a risk that you might fail, that you might be ridiculed, rejected, critiqued…that your creation might be damaged or destroyed or defaced.

That's what God did when he put on flesh and came to earth as a little baby named Jesus. He took the risk that his creation might be rejected (which it was) or that people might damage or even destroy what he had made (which they did). He took the risk that he himself, the great artist, the Lion of Judah, would bear the brunt of humanity's rejection.

God was willing to be unsafe with us.

Vulnerable with us.

He put all of himself into what he had made.

How Vulnerable Are You Willing to Get?

When I think about this concept of vulnerability, my good friend Mario comes to mind.

People often ask me who my favorite magician is. What a remarkably broad and difficult question with multiple layers of possible answers. That's like asking what's my favorite type of food. With so many varieties of food, the question really needs to be more specific. Favorite Italian food, Tex-Mex food, Thai food, Chinese food?

I could answer with a list of several names that, unless you follow the underground magic scene as geekily as I do, you probably have never heard of. But as I reflect through the list in my head,[78] one person continually rises to the top. Ironically, he is in my least favorite genre of magic: children's magic.

Mario: The Maker Magician.

In David Blaine's words, Mario is "the best children's magician in the world!" Mario is beyond creative and original. Even when he performs a classic trick in magic, it feels new and exciting. When a fellow magician friend told me I needed to catch Mario's show, I was super skeptical. Children's magic is often a hard pass for me. Yet, from the second Mario jumped on stage (literally jumped...or maybe purposely tripped), I was mesmerized by his creativity.

Over the last couple years, I have had the honor of forging a deep friendship with Mario, and I have finally figured out why he is so incredible. Every trick he does has so much of him in it. What you see onstage is simply...*Mario*. Every trick reeks of him.

He has so many original bits that I was surprised when he told me one day that he was writing a book that gave away

---

78   If you really want to know, DM me on your favorite social media.

all the magic secrets he had been developing over the last several years. Creations that were his babies, with countless hours of blood, sweat, and tears of creativity poured into them. And he was going to share and entrust them to anyone who would buy his book.

Pause. If you are not a magician, maybe you don't understand the gravity of his book writing. In magic, "the secret" is everything. Happening upon the ability to perform an illusion takes hours upon hours of work. And to then share these secrets with others is like sharing a part of your soul. A couple of close friends, sure. But with the general public? That's crazy talk.

While walking around his hometown of Nyack, New York, talking about his book release, he told me something amazing. He said that though he was scared to share all his secrets, to be so vulnerable with the general public, it was the greatest thing possible for him creatively.

After protecting his secret creations for so long, it was hard to see past them. But once he shared them, then it gave him a clean slate, a tabula rasa…a *brand new* blank composition notebook ready for *brand new* ideas!

And he was right. The new ideas that came after his book release were so innovative, so inventive, so bursting with breakthrough that he wishes he had shared the ideas so much earlier.

What if this is how we approached our life with God, knowing that the way we are living might not be God's best? Often, we are willing to give some of our life over, but we reserve parts that we are scared for anyone to know about. Our browser history? Things we have strived to fix in ourselves? The parts we keep trying to get right.

It's like God is holding his hands out asking, *How vulnerable are you willing to be with me? Are you willing to give me all your pursuits up till now?*

The real question God is asking is, *How much do you trust me?*

It is ridiculous how hard this is, right? If we should be completely vulnerable with anyone, it should be our Creator. The one who knows our thoughts deeper than we know them ourselves. And yet...that almost makes it so much scarier.

It reminds me of when the nation of Israel was wandering around in the desert after escaping the slavery of Egypt. God had just rescued the entire nation from their slave owners through magnificent displays of powerful signs and wonders. Yet when God's presence descended on Mount Sinai, the people had no desire to be near him:

> When the people saw the thunder and lightning and heard the trumpet and saw the mountain in smoke, they trembled with fear. They stayed at a distance and said to Moses, "Speak to us yourself and we will listen. But do not have God speak to us or we will die."
>
> Moses said to the people, "Do not be afraid. God has come to test you, so that the fear of God will be with you to keep you from sinning."

> The people remained at a distance, while Moses
> approached the thick darkness where God was.[79]

Here was God their Rescuer—ready to meet with them—and yet they withdrew. Why?

It's likely, isn't it, that they held back for one of same reasons that today we are scared of being completely vulnerable with God. In the presence of power, our weakness seems even weaker. In the presence of perfection, our imperfections seem so much more obvious. In the presence of stunning beauty, our blemishes seem weighty. It's like that moment when you have been inside all day with dim lighting and then you step outside and your eyes scream in pain from the brightness of the sun. As your pupils contract and you squint, desperately wishing you had remembered your sunglasses, you wonder if coming outside was worth it.

But we cannot stay inside forever.

If we want to live the best life possible and be the most creative, purposeful versions of ourselves, we must start by being open and vulnerable with God in every aspect of our lives.

---

79   Exodus 20:18–21, NIV.

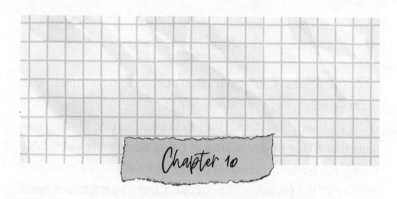

THE IGNORANT, UNEDUCATED ART CRITIC

When I envision an art critic, Anton Ego's face pops into my head. Ego is the food critic in the Pixar movie *Ratatouille*. The guy sits over the meal with those sunken eyes and that snooty snout, and he peers condescendingly down on his world. Ego is always ready to give a scathing review, and he's always certain that he knows better than everyone else.

Art critics can be the worst.

And they seem to flock like buzzards to Broadway.

The plays and musicals of Broadway are a love language for my wife and me. I know Gary Chapman says that there are only five love languages,[80] but I have performed at conferences with him, and in the green room, I respectfully told him that he forgot to mention the sixth one:

Broadway.

Just being in the theater district of New York City helps my wife and me reconnect and fall in love all over again. Therefore we plan as many trips to New York City as possible.

---

80 I love Gary Chapman's book, *The 5 Love Languages* (Chicago, IL: Moody Publishers, 2014). If you haven't read it and want a healthy relationship, you should read it.

We eat at our favorite restaurants, visit our favorite parks, but mostly we go to see musical theater. When the lights go down, the orchestra starts to play the overture, and her hand is in mine, it is the most incredible thing on this planet earth.

But there is a necessary evil in Broadway: the art critic. After opening night of every production, the casts gather together, eagerly awaiting the reviews to come out. The future of the show seems to depend on the good or bad reviews, on what these critics think about what happened on stage. Shows have opened and closed on the same day due to poor reviews.

And yet critics are needed. We need constructive, honest critique. We need educated people who have studied the art form they are commenting on to tell us the good and bad. We need educated critics to help us continue pushing art forward.

What we don't need are uneducated, ignorant critics speaking as if they are authorities in art. If I watch a dance routine, while I can tell you what made me smile or what moved me emotionally, I am not able to properly critique the dancer's form because I have no background in the fundamentals of dance.

In the age of Yelp and social media, everyone thinks they should comment/word vomit on everything, even if they have no knowledge on the subject. Out of this has also birthed the "trolls." The "trolls" are people throwing their negative opinions out as if they are the voice of a god, when they have no understanding of the art form or art medium being used. Often, they post negative or even hateful comments on stuff simply because they want to spew grossness. These are the critics I want to focus on.

MY PENN & TELLER: FOOL US
MAGIC FORMULA

COUNTLESS HOURS OF PRACTICE
➡️ **RUBIK'S CUBE** ⬅️

PAPER BAG
DESIRE TO MAKE FRIENDS
AND APPARENTLY, HAIR THAT "LOOKS LIKE A PINEAPPLE"

My National TV Debut

One of the highlights of my magic career was the privilege of appearing on the CW's hit show *Penn & Teller: Fool Us*. From the tech crew to the stars of the show, Penn Jillette and Raymond Teller, I loved every person and minute of the experience. When I finished my tricks, Penn and Teller had so many complimentary words for my act, to the point that at the end, they jumped up from their seats to shake my hand (something they rarely have done with other acts). It was exhilarating!

After the show aired, I recorded it and posted it to my YouTube channel. Everyone who cared about me reminded me of what I already knew. When you post something on YouTube…

Beware of the trolls! Don't read the comments.

But how do you not?

YouTube sends you an email notification every time someone posts a comment. If you go to the video, you will see that 90 percent of the comments are super nice and encouraging. The other 10 percent of comments can be grouped into categories that don't really pertain to me or who I truly am (as a person or a performer).

The critical comments ran the gamut. There were mean-spirited theories on how the tricks were done. Some people were confused about why Teller didn't talk. There were comments from speed Cubers who were annoyed because they didn't understand that this was a magic show and not a Rubik's Cube competition. And, believe it or not, there were weird and brutal comments about my hair and fingernails.

My life is an open book here. Or, I should say, an open YouTube page. Go check it out.

Here are some of my favorites about my hair:

- With hair like that, this guy needs every "opportunity for a relationship" he can get.
- What a talented pineapple.
- Dude's got skills but still looks like an iced gem.
- Did he do his haircut with a vacuum cleaner?
- Sadly enough, the haircut is no magic…it is there to stay for a while.
- Didn't know SpongeBob's house can do magic.
- The poop emoji on his head is very distracting.

- Penn finally changed his hair. This guy needs to do the same. Wow. It's his best use of misdirection.
- So this is what Jimmy Neutron is doing these days.

Sticks and stones…
But words will…
Agggghhhh.
Of course, hurtful words hurt. How can they not?

And here's the worst part about all those comments. In an effort to revisit those comments in order to find them to list here, I now feel like junk. Truly ick. Which is stupid because I know they come from uneducated trolls. And yet they still made me feel like trash all over again. The majority of comments on my video affirm how entertaining and positive my performance was. And yet, my mind gravitates toward the vitriol. What would your mind do? Are you like me? Would you be tempted to let a few mean comments obscure the overwhelming mass of kind ones?

This is a struggle for most of us.

Most research has shown that people generally need at least five positive comments to make up for every bad one. A five-to-one ratio.

I think I need a ninety-nine-to-one ratio.

And yet, that one negative comment still crushes me.

Again.

Again.

And what if there are more than one?

Again and again…and again.

The problem for a lot of creatives is that the bad ones just keep sneaking back around and hitting you when you're least suspecting it.

This is how hurtful or debasing comments work, right? One disrespectful word, and all of the encouraging ones seem to disappear into thin air. That one dumb comment echoes in the lonely caverns of the brain over and over. The tractor-beam pull toward the comments seems too strong to resist. And over and over, the lies plant seeds and grow within.

All those YouTube comments, the good and the bad, are from ignorant, uneducated art critics. I'm all for feedback from my audiences that view my shows, but the vast majority of them have not spent years studying the art form of magic.

Of all the comments on my performance, the reviews that should matter to me are those of Penn and Teller.[81] There is a reason they have their own TV show reviewing other magicians. They have spent decades performing and studying the art form of magic. Their comments and opinions are

---

81 Who had nothing but incredibly nice and complimentary things to say.

not ignorant or uneducated. Their words should carry more weight when it comes to how I performed on the show.

"Poiema"

Early on in my performing arts and speaking career, my wife designed a T-shirt for my merch table to fight against this sort of swirling negativity and lies. It has been one of the main messages I give at the end of my shows. Maribeth drew this amazing traditional card deck spade and artistically included the following words:

"I'm a Masterpiece."

What a great reminder.

This phrase is not a throw-away feel-goodism for millennials and Gen Z. It's not a participation award. It's not some kind of a self-help, personal motivation speech. No, this is what God thinks.

About me.

About you.

This is based on what the apostle Paul wrote to the church in Ephesus. He wrote:

> For we are God's masterpiece. He has created us anew in Christ Jesus, so we can do the good things he planned for us long ago.[82]

The word *masterpiece* can also be translated "workmanship" or "handiwork." As in we are God's workmanship like the Sistine Chapel was Michelangelo's handiwork. The Greek word that is being translated is *poiema*.

Poiema.

---

82 Ephesians 2:10, NLT.

Sound like anything?

Where we get our English word, you guessed it, *poem.*

We are God's poetry.

His artwork.

His masterpiece.

And I love that God declares us his *poiema,* his "poem." In a way, we are made with the same kind of intentionality he used to communicate our origin story way back in Genesis. I love it when art has unlimited depths to explore.

I have shared a version of this message all over the world at youth camps, retreats, and even as a part of my magic shows. Maribeth's design declares to the T-shirt wearer and to everyone who sees the shirt that no matter how they view themselves or how others view them, if they are in Christ, they have been remade into God's masterpiece.

There's Always That One Persistent, Critical Bully

Pro-tip.

This one is free with the book.

A bonus bit.

If one wants to launch a career in the performing arts like the career I have, it would be much easier to start in one's early twenties. That way, perhaps they'd not yet be married nor have children and would find it simpler to live on little to nothing and go crash on friends' couches as needed.

Maribeth and I launched into this career when I was thirty-two. We were married with two children. As a family, we'd been paying the bills from my youth pastor salary and missionary earnings. At the time we were not planning or expecting to launch this magic/speaking career. Therefore, we had no savings in the bank to back us up. But when we found ourselves at a career crossroads in our life, we realized we were being presented with an interesting opportunity. My wife and I looked at each other knowingly, as if to say, "If we don't at least give this a shot, we will always wonder, *what if?*"

The only way we could afford to launch this career was to move our entire family into the upstairs of my parents' home.

My. Parents'. Home.

Did I mention I was thirty-two?

Did I mention I was married with two kids?

Did I mention my parents' home?

Did I mention I was thirty-two?

<Slap to the face!>

It was one of the most humbling things I have ever done. When you are in your early thirties and have owned a home, have been supplying for all your family's needs, and have lived overseas with them, the last thing you expect to do is to move back in with Mommy and Daddy.

Beyond emasculating for a grown man.

My "office" became the local Starbucks. We prayed, hustled, and tried to do anything and everything we possibly could to turn the dream of doing magic and speaking into something that could support our family. We even set up a makeshift photography studio in our temporary bedroom to create promotional materials and videos. Honestly, most days were pretty discouraging, and most of the time I didn't know what I was going to do when I "went back to work" every morning.

The biggest bully in my life didn't stop bothering me in grade school like most of the others. To this day, he still follows me around constantly. He even stares at me when I brush my teeth every morning.

It's me.

Not some creepy stalker dude.

It's me.

I'm my biggest bully.

One morning, as I was starting on the top right row of my teeth, the bully came out of nowhere and started really laying into me.

First, a body blow about my physical appearance. How I had too much "love" in my "love handles." How the many pimples or other problems I had with my face looked so gross.

Then he threw some uppercuts on how I had failed as a father, as a husband, and as a man.

> *A man in his thirties shouldn't have to have someone else paying his bills. He should be able to provide for his family's needs. You are such a loser!*

Then he landed some brutal headshots on my relationship with my Creator.

> *You know, you don't take enough time to read the Bible or pray. You think you represent him? Huh? Really?*

After about ten to fifteen minutes of my bully staring at me and tearing me down in the mirror, I was to the point of audibly cussing myself out.

But for a moment I broke through the bully and made eye contact with my real self.

And then I noticed what shirt I was wearing.

"I'm a Masterpiece."

Hold on now.

Halt everything.

I looked up from the shirt and made eye contact with myself again. I just stared blankly. How could I ever declare that a creation of the greatest artist ever was "trash"?

God doesn't make junk.

God doesn't even make mediocre.

God doesn't even make pretty good.

God makes a masterpiece.

Poiema.

I realized the truth: that I had become an ignorant, uneducated art critic. Yes, a troll of one of God's masterpieces. This message I have shared to hundreds at youth camps is the message I still need to hear every day.

Get Rid of the Labels

Remember the verse Maribeth made into a shirt? Kind of central to the book theme:

> For we are God's masterpiece. He has created us
> anew in Christ Jesus, so we can do the good things he
> planned for us long ago.[83]

In the sentences that follow it, Paul carries the thought into overcoming the labels that separate us from who Christ calls us to be. Because we are God's masterpiece, because we have been created anew in Christ, because we can do the good things he planned for us, we don't have to live under the burden of lies and labels anymore.

---

83   Ephesians 2:10, NLT.

For his readers, Paul calls out the labels he knew had been thrown on them:

Outsiders

Unclean

Non-citizens

Apart

Excluded

Without God

Without hope

Paul was writing to non-Jews in this letter to the church in Ephesus. Gentiles. There was deep-seated racism and labels that ran deep in the time and culture of this letter. Roman gentiles ruled over and often brutalized Jewish people. Jews would not even eat a meal with gentiles as then they would be considered "unclean" if they came into contact with the "gross uncircumcised people."

So, Paul, after showing how these gentiles are also "God's masterpiece" created in Christ, now addresses the elephant in the room. "Look," he says, "I know people have put these labels on you. But the truth is this":

> Now you have been united with Christ Jesus. Once you were far away from God, but now you have been brought near to him through the blood of Christ.[84]

Maybe other people have been your ignorant critics.

Or maybe you've been your own troll.

No matter who has been putting those negative voices in your ears and that blurred vision in your eyes and those

---

84 Ephesians 2:13, NLT.

deflating thoughts in your head, it is only what Jesus says about you that really matters.

Let's get rid of those labels right now. It doesn't matter what labels you or anyone else put on you in the past. The only one whose opinion matters is the *most* educated on the matter. The artist. The Creator. And he not only loves you, but he also actually likes you. Wants to share your company. Wants to hang with you. Thinks you are worth his time.

Are you willing to accept that though? When the lies about your worth from uneducated trolls speak loudly in your head, are you willing to combat them with God's opinion of you?

Give yourself permission to be re-labeled by the Expert. Listen to the right voice. Put up a sticky note on your bathroom mirror.

God doesn't make trash.

You are God's poem.

You are God's creation.

You are God's masterpiece!

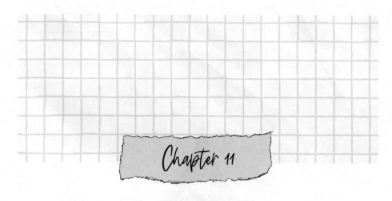

DO THE IMPOSSIBLE!

"How did you do that?"

That's a question magicians hear a lot.

But if I'm honest, I feel like that is the wrong question.

When I think about doing magic tricks, the exact technique of "how" is not actually the most impressive thing to me. A better question is, "How did someone decide to do *that* trick?" How did someone discover that producing a rabbit from a top hat would be amazing to people? How did someone land upon the idea that we should saw a lady in half? How did someone decide to turn a Rubik's Cube into Skittles?[85] To come up with a cool trick that appears to be magic that people will want to watch…*that* is the interesting part of magic.

As I already talked about, coming up with new magic tricks is one of the hardest things I do. It seems that there is nothing new in the art of magic. Coming up with even a small nuance on a classic trick can be incredible for a magician's career. Whenever a new take on a classic trick is accomplished, the magic community freaks out about it. In our

---

85 This trick happens in every one of my live shows.

magician circles, the process of getting there earns someone his or her street cred. And honor is given when everyone else starts mimicking it.

That's cool. But new takes aren't new tricks. They're great and exciting. But I long for the day when the nothing-new cycle stops reciprocating.

Walt with His Imagineers

When I think about "how" someone could "create something new," I think about Disney's Imagineers.

To say I am a fan of Disney is to say Babe Ruth might have been good at baseball. From growing up on all the classic films to spending hours glued to the Disney Channel to navigating every inch of the theme parks—if the Mouse is involved, I'm fully in. Through our fifteen-plus years of marriage, my wife and I have held constant annual passes at either Disneyland, Disneyland Paris, or Disney World.

Above the tunnel entrance of Disneyland, there is a plaque that reads, "Here you leave today and enter the world of yesterday, tomorrow and fantasy." Every time I walk through the tunnel, I feel that its promise is true. How did they convince me of that?

The idea of a theme park was not original to Walt Disney. But he is the one who took the idea to a completely new orbit. How did he convince teams of people to join his vision? How did he gather armies of dreamers and designers on his side?

The Imagineers.

If you are even a tenth of a Disney-dork as I am, you probably have heard of the Disney "Imagineers."

The Imagineers were created by Walt himself to be his idea-into-reality team. They became especially important when he launched his theme park. Their job was to take Walt's fantastical vision and make it a reality on the ground in the actual world.

And Walt had some big ideas:

- Let's create a castle that looks enormous.
- Let's make ghosts appear in the cars guests are riding in.
- Let's create a huge treehouse people can walk through.
- Let's create a monorail.
- Let's take people to Neverland on a pirate ship.
- Let's create an African safari in America.
- Let's take people under the sea with a hot crustacean band.

Imagination + Engineers = Imagineers. Their job is to take ideas born in fantasy and then figure out the physics and engineering to bring the idea to life in the theme parks. In other words, if Walt thought up and drew a small elephant with big floppy ears who could fly, the Imagineers were challenged to create a small elephant with big floppy ears who could fly. And if Walt said he wanted guests to ride in that elephant through the air…well, then…these guys had to figure it out. They had to organize the logistics of mechanics and design and safety and efficient influxes of crowds.

In more modern times, if the creative team at Disney says they want a huge fire-breathing dragon to be part of the parade that goes down Main Street, the Imagineers jump into action. First, the Imagineers have to figure out how to make a fully functional fire-breathing dragon. Then they must consider how it will fit in the narrow route the parade takes. And then they must consider how its fire breath could be so safe that no guest would ever be hurt or burned if something were to happen.

The Imagineers under Walt Disney have an ethic that drives them. They always want to "Plus It!" Putting something out that is "good enough" is never acceptable. The team is always challenged to continue to creatively and collaboratively innovate and improve upon their projects.

It's kind of fun to do the impossible.

— walt disney

My buddy Mark is a retired Imagineer. Overcoming "impossible" was his daily job. He told me that when Disney wanted to create the "Baymax at Hiro's Workshop" meet-and-greet experience at EPCOT, they ran into a huge problem with the costume. Baymax is the futuristic robot from the animated movie *Big Hero Six*. On the screen, the animated Baymax seems to be made out of a vinyl-looking material, but in reality, you can't make something like Baymax out of vinyl that will look and act the way it needs to and be durable enough to withstand all the guest interactions and the Florida heat and humidity. So, my buddy's team of fellow Imagineers had to literally invent a new material. They combined three different types of fabrics to fit the requirements. With this new material, the look and feel that everyone imagines Baymax to have would actually be right.

Another story Mark told me was of how he was once tasked by the Disney designers to create an environment for a "princess" meet-and-greet experience. They envisioned a large, flowing waterfall that people could touch. But there was a catch. The filtration systems and pumps required to make the water safe for guests to touch was going to cost too much. They wanted a *waterless* waterfall. A waterfall…but without the key ingredient: water. Impossible. So, my friend's team came up with the idea of using tiny beads that look like water droplets to create the illusion of water that would be cycled just like water but wouldn't need the expensive filtration systems.

Often, young, brand-new engineers on my friend's team would hear an idea (like a waterfall without water) and laugh it off like it was impossible. But they learned quickly that if the Imagineers would have done that with every idea that came across the board, there would be no Disneyland or Disney World. No Space Mountain, no Pirates of the Caribbean, no audio-animatronics, and we'd have no great moments with Mr. Lincoln as he stands up to deliver the Gettysburg Address seemingly of his own accord.[86]

---

86 I'm a huge *Star Wars* fan. So, one of my favorite insights my buddy Mark has given me is this: When Disney opened up Galaxy's Edge, they wanted the Storm Troopers to be able to talk to people when they walked

They are a team of people dedicated to making the impossible possible. Over the years, Disney had a motto: "If it can be dreamt, it can be built."

What a bland reality this would be without the Imagineers.

This is the reason for this story: the purpose of the Imagineers was to help Disney make his vision a reality in this world. That is just like our role. Our purpose is to make God's vision for this world a reality.

Walt Disney couldn't have created everything on his own. He needed Imagineers. But God? God could simply do it all if he wanted. He's proven that already. But God wants us to be a part of his engineering design team. He wants us to be part of his innovative solutions and dynamic experiences. He wants us to share the joy of seeing people discover wonder and hope.

God could have just accomplished everything on his own, but he chose to employ us. He loves working together as a team. Throughout the Bible, God invites small bands of Imagineers into his grand vision. After Jesus rose from the grave, he gathered his followers, painted the picture in their minds of what they could do, gave them his Spirit, and commissioned them. "All over the world, for generations, I will empower you to be my witnesses," he told them, "I want you to make this world into the beautiful place of life and wonder that I created it to be."[87]

---

among the guests. So they developed a myriad of different phrases that are associated with their head motions and hand gestures to respond to guests, triggered by Bluetooth sensors in each of the Storm Trooper's costumes to enable collaborative conversations with other coordinated Troopers.

87 See Acts 1:1–11, 2:1–21; Matthew 28:18–20. In John 20:22–23, Jesus commissions his team of "Imagineers" by "breathing on them." At

Doing the Impossible with Rubik's Cubes

I have always been fascinated by Rubik's Cubes. The three-by-three-by-three squared puzzle often stumps people. It can seem so simple yet impossible—and that captivates me.

Since the toy came out in 1974, magicians have been using it for magic tricks. In 1982, the great Doug Henning performed an instant solving Rubik's Cube in his TV special, *Magic on Broadway*. He not only amazed his audience but fooled every magician who saw it. That cube trick was so innovative, yet it was basically the only "new" trick done with a cube for the next thirty to forty years.

But in the last six years, magic done with Rubik's Cubes has exploded. When Steven Brundage performed on *Penn &*

creation, Adam received life when God breathed into his nostrils (Genesis 2). In Ezekiel's vision, the dry bones in the valley received life when the Spirit breathed on them (Ezekiel 37). Do you feel like you need God's breath in you today?

Teller: Fool Us and later *America's Got Talent,* he ignited a new wave of attempts to create innovative tricks with the Rubik's Cube. Some magicians, mostly from Japan and Hong Kong, had already been dreaming up new ways to manipulate it, but Steven made it mainstream.

After reading about the new boom in doing magic with Rubik's Cubes, I took the square toy to my magic club with a challenge to come up with something new. I wanted to figure out a completely new concept for a cube trick that had never been done before. Little did I know, but that motivation would give birth to the trick that landed me on my first national TV appearance.

The elite magic club I belong to is called Sleight Club. The first rule of Sleight Club is "Don't suck."

The other big rule in Sleight Club is you are never allowed to say, "Well I know it plays…" This phrase is often the excuse of a lazy magician. The magician who uses this phrase is often not willing to put in the hours of practice needed or is simply accepting of a trick being "good enough." Our club is never happy with "good enough" or with magic that just "plays." We desire to elevate the art form of magic as high as it can go. If a trick is good but has a couple of awkward moments where a move needs to happen, we don't just hope the audience doesn't catch it. Instead, we will keep working, keep thinking, until we have developed the best trick.

The Sleight Club was brainstorming innovative tricks with a cube when one member sparked, "You know what would be cool? What if you took all the stickers off like everyone does, and then magically put them back on."

Boom!

I know you are sitting there reading this just dumb-founded. Your mind has been melted with the brilliance of this statement, right? Well, okay. You probably don't care even a fraction as much about this idea as I did that night. Maybe it seems small or insignificant to you. But in my world, I can't tell you how excited I got sitting around that table at that moment.

Because this was a trick, a concept in magic, that no one had ever thought of or performed before.

And we didn't know how it could be done.

At first.

But together we *imagined*.

And we found a way.

It was a killer method.

I worked and worked on the trick, and then I filmed it in my office and posted it online. When the magic community saw my video, I started getting messages from all over the world, including from the producers of *Penn & Teller: Fool Us*.

Don't Settle

When we take the time to put in the extra effort,

when we strive for the "best,"

when we don't settle for "good enough,"

it's amazing what can happen.

And I think that what we all want is God's best for us.

So why do we so often give in to this desire to settle for "good enough"? Why would we stop searching, stop seeking, stop innovating? Why would we rather be lazy and sit on the couch with a bag of chips?

In the eyewitness account of the book of Matthew, the apostle describes an encounter between a rich man and Jesus.[88] The rich man approached Jesus and asked,

"Teacher, what *good* deed must I do to have eternal life?"

Jesus responded curiously to the man.

" 'Why ask me about what is good?' Jesus replied. 'There is only One who is good.' "

The rich man had asked Jesus, "What is 'good enough'? What is the minimum requirement? What is the least amount of effort I need to put in for this to play out?"

Jesus, so witty and surprising and ready, tells the man to do something that seemed simply impossible for him.

"If you want to be perfect, here's what you need to do."

The story ends sadly with the rich ruler walking away, depressed but not willing or able to do what was required for "God's best." The disciples also could not believe all that they had heard. When the ruler walked away, Jesus turned to them and said:

"I tell you the truth, it is very hard for a rich person to enter the Kingdom of Heaven. I'll say it again—it is easier for a camel to go through the eye of a needle than for a rich person to enter the Kingdom of God!"

This statement blew their minds. We cannot fully understand how much of their gray matter was destroyed unless we understand that their cultural concept of being "rich" was tied directly to the spiritual idea that "God had blessed you." The only way to have God bless you is if you made him happy with you. This was not just a Jewish belief. All the religious beliefs of the day held that the only way you would have wealth was if you had pleased the gods and they, in turn, blessed you with fortune.

---

88 Matthew 19:16–30, NLT (emphasis added).

So put yourself in their shoes. If this was what you assumed to be true and then Jesus said that it is basically impossible for a rich person to enter the kingdom of heaven, then what chance would there be for the rest of us "ordinary" non-rich people?

That is why the eyewitness account of Matthew continues with the disciples incredulously responding to Jesus: "Then who in the world can be saved?"

To which Jesus replies, "Not you. It's impossible."

Ha! Thanks, Jesus. Thank you for this encouraging sermon.

No, listen. Jesus says, "Humanly speaking, it is impossible. But with God everything is possible."

Boom!

We can strive all we want in our own power. We can accumulate as much stuff as we can get our arms and credit cards around. We can get all the social media likes and reposts. We can try to work hard and acquire all the fancy brands of shoes and cars. But on our own—no matter how much we try to spin it—it will only just be…okay.

Not the best.

Why settle for something blah when you could have the best possible version of God's creation? Even if it seems an impossible feat for someone like you, the first set of three words are life-changing:

"But with God…"

They are life-changing because they lead us to the second set of three words:

"Everything is possible."

So, don't settle.

It's time to *imaginate* with God.

Chapter 12

LET'S COLLAB!

COLLAB

noun
/kə'læb/

short for collaboration:

a situation in which two or more people work together to create, achieve, or promote (encourage people to buy or use) something.

EXAMPLE:

virtually everyone I have worked with so far, or linked in with on collabs, is abroad, and we've never met.

89 Cambridge Dictionary, s.v. "collab," accessed December 13, 2021, https://

Why This Book Ever Even Happened

I have tried to write a book in the past…and failed.

Actually, I once wrote a book. But, strangely, in the process, I learned that I don't have the ability to write in my own voice. Weird, right?

I tried…again and again. But though I am a decent public speaker, whenever I tried to put those same words down on paper, something just didn't jive. I have humbly accepted the fact that I will never be a Hemingway, C. S. Lewis, or Tolkien.[90]

So when a friend, Ken Castor, approached me at a youth conference in 2018 and suggested I write a book, I laughed. Been there. Done that. Moved on without too much embarrassment. I told him what I had told many other people: "I've tried and failed."

But Ken, who just might be the best guy ever, persisted.[91] He asked if I had ever tried a collab approach to writing. I told him I had heard of "ghost writing" in the past but honestly thought it would be "cheating" or that it was only something big time celebrities with lots of money did when they wanted to write their memoirs. Ken explained to me that though there are "ghost writers" who do write for celebrities, there are also co-writing ventures, where you take the content and thoughts of one writer and team them up with a more seasoned writer to get out a message.

And this is what you have in your hands right now. A true collaboration of thoughts and ideas. Written equally by two authors to get one message out to the world.

Honestly, I thought this would be a lot less work on my end. Ha! Originally, I hoped that I could just have Ken

dictionary.cambridge.org/us/dictionary/english/collab.
90 Though I do envy their classy fashion.
91 I'm not sure exactly, but I think Ken might have written this sentence.

interview me, and then he would write the whole thing. But that's not how it worked. Turns out that I spent countless hours writing thousands upon thousands of words. On airplanes. In hotel rooms. In my office. Often while listening to Miles Davis, John Coltrane, Dean Martin, and Frank Sinatra. And Ken would spend countless hours coming alongside to polish it and fill it and shape it into the readable manuscript that all of you see before you.

At one point, Ken came down to Texas, stayed in my magic speakeasy of an office,[92] ate with my family, listened to my geek session on card decks, picked up my son from school, and helped me buy diapers and Cheez-Its from Walmart.

Though ghost writing might have been easier for me, I have actually loved this partnership process. It is a mutual invitation of trust. It is a reciprocal, vulnerable commitment.

It is truly a collab of both our talents.

⸔ MAGIC TRICKS JOHN'S FRIEND KEN ⸕ HAS ~~PERFECTED~~ BEEN WORKING ON
JOHN DID NOT TEACH KEN THESE

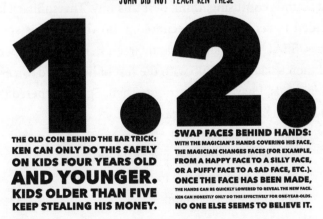

1.
THE OLD COIN BEHIND THE EAR TRICK: **KEN CAN ONLY DO THIS SAFELY ON KIDS FOUR YEARS OLD AND YOUNGER. KIDS OLDER THAN FIVE KEEP STEALING HIS MONEY.**

2.
SWAP FACES BEHIND HANDS: WITH THE MAGICIAN'S HANDS COVERING HIS FACE, THE MAGICIAN CHANGES FACES (FOR EXAMPLE, FROM A HAPPY FACE TO A SILLY FACE, OR A PUFFY FACE TO A SAD FACE, ETC.). **ONCE THE FACE HAS BEEN MADE,** THE HANDS CAN BE QUICKLY LOWERED TO REVEAL THE NEW FACE. KEN CAN HONESTLY ONLY DO THIS EFFECTIVELY FOR ONE-YEAR-OLDS. **NO ONE ELSE SEEMS TO BELIEVE IT.**

---

92   If you wonder what a magic speakeasy office looks like, check out my socials and you'll see it.

This is how I think God has always intended the world to be. Collaboration with each other is God's plan A for how the world should operate. And there was no plan B. In other words, he did not have nor want any other plan. This was it.

The Collaborative Path

One of the greatest stories of collaboration is embedded within God's plan A for Moses and Israel.

Do you remember Moses' story? It was told to me in a Sunday school room on flannel graphs. It was also told to me in the animated movie *The Prince of Egypt*. God had just rescued the Israelites from the Egyptians with a devastatingly awe-inspiring display of power through the ten plagues rained on Egypt.[93]

As the Israelites were leaving Egypt, Pharaoh (the king of Egypt) decided to grab his army and go after Israel. Pharaoh "took with him 600 of Egypt's best chariots, along with the rest of the chariots of Egypt, each with its commander."[94]

Wait, six hundred of his best chariots plus the rest? If that sounds confusing, think of it this way. This military king decided to send his best technology in warfare—his special forces, SEAL teams, snipers, and Green Beret paratroopers—and then backed them up with the rest of his armed forces. In other words, Pharaoh was serious. Then, Egypt cornered their lost slaves against the Red Sea.

The fight was over.

Israel was outmatched and outgunned.

They had nowhere else to run.

Their doom was certain.

---

93 Find in Exodus chapters 7–11.
94 Exodus 14:7, NLT.

Realizing this, God's people cried out to Moses, "Didn't we tell you this would happen while we were still in Egypt? We said, 'Leave us alone! Let us be slaves to the Egyptians. It's better to be a slave in Egypt than a corpse in the wilderness!' "[95]

What happens next is why movies and books are still being made about this story from the Jewish Scriptures. God told Moses to stretch out his staff over the Red Sea.

That's God's big plan.

To hold a walking stick out over an ocean.

So, Moses collaborated. He vulnerably trusted and participated.

He held out the stick.

An east wind blew in and split the sea.

With humans, it is impossible. But with God…

A dry path to freedom with an alarmingly beautiful wall of water on both sides. An unequalled aquarium view on the right and on the left. The Israelites crossed through the sea and escaped from their certain death.

Meanwhile, the super technologically advanced Egyptian army pursued them on the path through the sea. But Pharaoh's advanced technology was no match for God. The wheels of the chariots jammed in the mud. The horses lost their minds. And the Egyptian army remembered they were not just fighting Israelite slaves; they were also fighting Israel's God. They exclaimed, "Let's get out of here—away from these Israelites… The LORD is fighting for them against Egypt!"[96] But after every Israelite had safely crossed, God told Moses to again stretch out his staff. Moses did, and the walls of water crashed together, drowning and destroying all of the Egyptian army.

---

95   Exodus 14:12, NLT.
96   Exodus 14:25, NLT.

The Jewish Scriptures end this story by saying:

> When the people of Israel saw the mighty power that the LORD had unleashed against the Egyptians, they were filled with awe before him. They put their faith in the LORD and in his servant Moses.[97]

You, like me, have probably heard this story many times. But rereading it recently made me pause.

There's a major part of the story that doesn't make sense. A part of the story that is not needed.

The plagues are needed to tell the story.

The slaves escaping are crucial to the story.

The Pharaoh's stubbornness is necessary.

The roadblock of the sea is needed.

God's rescue is most definitely essential.

God overwhelming Pharaoh's "advanced" technology is key.

The closure of the sea is a slam dunk.

All of those things are necessary elements to the events of this famous story. But what detail of this story is not really necessary? And yet highlighted?

Moses stretching out his staff.

Seriously, Moses stretching out his walking stick is not necessary. Have you ever tried stretching out a stick at a body of water? I have. Nothing happens. There is not a scientific reaction when walking sticks are stretched out toward bodies of water. It is not like when you combine Mentos and Coke or baking soda and peroxide. Moses stretching out his staff does nothing by itself.

So why did God tell Moses to do it? God did not need Moses to stretch out his staff. God wasn't a genie, and Moses

97   Exodus 14:31, NLT.

wasn't Aladdin. God did not need Moses to say, "Genie, I wish for…" in order for God to act.

So why did God ask Moses to do it? In fact, why did God include Moses at all?

Because collaboration with humans is God's plan A for this world. Over and over again in the collected library of books called the Bible, you'll see God patiently waiting for humankind to work with him before acting. God doesn't need our participation to act. But he wants it. And over and over again, he patiently waits for us to collab with him to accomplish his will.

God patiently waits for us.

God patiently waits for you.

And if that isn't cool enough, did you catch the end of the parting of the Red Sea story? God shares the credit. Check this out:

"They put their faith in the LORD and in his servant Moses."[98]

Wait, what? Yes, of course the Israelites put their faith in God. He had just split an ocean! Even the Egyptian army recognized whose power was on display with that one. But why should Moses receive any credit?

Are you following how crazy this is? God displays his power and receives the glory due. But he isn't scared or jealous of allowing the Israelites to also put their trust in Moses.

Look, if you did the majority of the work and let someone who had no power in and of himself to do a menial task as part of the project (like, I don't know, let's say, he held up a stick…), how would you feel if you had to share the glory with him at the awards ceremony?

---

98 Exodus 14:31, NLT.

It reminds me of when I used to help my dad carry heavy objects. Did you ever do this? Did your dad ever let you "help" by putting a hand or finger on the object as he and another adult actually carried the object? Honestly, as I look back on those moments, it probably made the tasks more cumbersome for my dad. It would have been much easier for my dad and the other adults if I had just stayed out of the way. Yet, my dad included me, just as I now let my own kids "help" me. Why?

Because I like doing things with my kids.

Just like my dad liked doing things with me.

As stated earlier, God doesn't need us to accomplish anything in this universe. Yet he has chosen that this is his plan. To the point that he has entrusted it into our hands.

After Jesus rose from the dead, he was on earth for forty more days. Some of his last words reaffirmed that a collab is his only desire and only plan for the redemption of this world. He told his followers:

> "I have been given all authority in heaven and on earth. Therefore, go and make disciples of all the nations, baptizing them in the name of the Father and the Son and the Holy Spirit. Teach these new disciples to obey all the commands I have given you."[99]

Oh, then he also added a reminder that we are not alone:

"And be sure of this: I am with you always, even to the end of the age."[100]

In other words, Jesus has the all the authority and power and presence to do it all by himself, but where would be the fun be in that?[101]

---

99 Matthew 28:18–20, NLT.
100 Matthew 28:20, NIV.
101 It must have been fun for God to see a small band of Imagineers filled

Ego: The Imaginate Killer

It's a group project! I'm curious if you got excited or cringed when I brought up the subject.

When you have to do a group project, who are you in the group? Are you the worried, micro-managing student who is making sure others don't screw up your grade? Are you the lazy one who lets everyone else do the work? Or are you the quiet one who will work way too hard letting others take advantage of you while you inwardly grow more and more bitter? Or are you the team player who brings out the best in each participant? Whether in school or the workplace, group projects either produce the greatest ideas or a broken relationship with a poor output.

The biggest enemy of collaboration isn't a lack of creativity; it is ego. When everyone is mutually focused on the purpose of the collaboration, beautiful things can happen. But as soon as someone thinks he is better than others in the group or as soon as someone wants more credit for himself, everything starts to break down.

Group projects teach us the following rules about life:

- Don't be selfish.
- Don't try to impress others.
- Be humble, thinking of others as better than yourself.
- Don't look out only for your own interests but take an interest in others.[102]

I have a singer-songwriter friend who has worked with some of the biggest names in the music industry. He has

with his Spirit begin to boldly spread his good news around the world.

102 Paul shared these rules over two thousand years ago. See Philippians 2:3–4. Then in v. 5, he adds, "You must have the same attitude that Christ Jesus had" (NLT).

collaborated to write and produce several Grammy Award–winning songs with incredibly talented artists. He told me that during a songwriting collaboration, if both artists keep focused on creating a song that gets a message out to the world, then it will be successful. But as soon as one artist tries to take over the project or push his own agenda or make a name for himself (over the other person), the entire session falls apart.

God set the boundaries for group projects in the garden of Eden. It was to be a beautiful partnership of the *God collab* and humankind working together, creating together. Utopia. But ego got in the way. Humankind's ego said, "We know better than God." And then all hell, literally, broke loose on earth.

Since it was in a group project that humanity screwed up, it makes sense that God would initiate a group project to create a solution.

22 WAYS
to Collab with God

SEE AT LEAST ONE NEW THING GOD CREATED EVERY DAY. WRITE IT IN A JOURNAL.

ASK YOURSELF: WHAT DOES LOVE REQUIRE OF ME?

WHEN YOU SEE CHAOS, EXPLORE CREATIVE SOLUTIONS FOR PEACE.

THINK AHEAD ONE HOUR. WHAT COULD YOU DO TO REPRESENT GOD BEST?

SING.

WRITE A POEM ABOUT THE SKIES.

MAKE A COLLAGE OF PICTURES WITH TREE BRANCHES AS THE SUBJECT.

SEND A LONELY FRIEND AN ENCOURAGING NOTE.

START YOUR DAY BY ASKING GOD WHAT HE HAS GOING ON TODAY.

WRITE "I AM A MASTERPIECE" ON A STICKY NOTE AND PUT IT ON YOUR BATHROOM MIRROR.

GIVE PEOPLE SOMETHING MORE CREATIVE THAN A TYPICAL GREETING TODAY.

CELEBRATE SOMEONE WHO HAS DONE GOOD WORK WITHOUT MUCH FANFARE.

TAKE A STEP TO PRACTICE A SKILLSET YOU HAVEN'T USED MUCH YET.

PUT PHILIPPIANS 4:8 IN YOUR HEAD.

GO FOR A WALK.

INVITE THE NEXT GENERATION TO DISCOVER CREATIVITY.

STOP LISTENING TO FEAR; START SPEAKING HOPE.

LOOK FOR GOD'S STORY IN EVERY STORY.

SPEND THIRTY MINUTES THINKING ABOUT THE VASTNESS OF CREATION.

SPEND THIRTY MINUTES THINKING ABOUT THE INTRICACIES OF CREATION.

GET A WATERCOLOR NOTEPAD & A CHEAP ROW OF WATERCOLORS. FILL THE NOTEPAD IN ONE WEEK.

HANG OUT WITH FRIENDS WHO INSPIRE YOU.

BEST WAY TO IMAGINATE WITH GOD.

So how do we *imaginate* with God?

First, what talents do you have?

Jesus told a story about how a master entrusted "talents" (or money) to his three servants before a long trip.[103] When the master returned, two of the three were creative with what had been entrusted to them. They had invested the money and gained more for their master. But one of the servants was scared to do anything with what was entrusted to him, so he simply buried it in the ground. The ones who were creative, the master rewarded with more. As for the one who did nothing, even the little he had was taken away.

One of my mentors used to say, "If you do a lot with a little, someday you'll get to do a lot with a lot. But if you do a little with a little, you'll lose the little you got."[104]

This parable makes me think about Thrivent Financial. I get to perform for a lot of corporate clients, so I get to see a variety of companies behind the scenes. One of my favorites is Thrivent—a financial institution whose goal is for its members not to just be financially secure and have financial clarity but to also be able to live generously. Think about that. A financial institution that is all about banking and buying

---

103 You can find this story in Matthew 25:14–30.
104 Neil Kelly, you got this phrase stuck in my head. I don't know if you came up with it or stole it from someone, but thank you for introducing it to me.

and selling stocks and life insurance but whose goal is for their people to give away their money. They do this because they believe money is a tool, not a goal. This is so creative and collaborative! They believe that by using their "talents" to spread love, joy, and support, they will spur other talents in this world. So, they invest and grow money to be able to give it away generously. Just like what is said in the musical *Hello Dolly*, "Money...is like manure. It's not worth a thing unless it's spread around, encouraging young things to grow."

Everyone has been given talents. I'm no longer talking about just your finances but rather any gifts and abilities you possess. Maybe it's your raw talent. Or maybe it's a learned skill. Whether you feel like you have an unending well of talents or whether you wonder if the talent parade skipped your street, you have the ability to do amazing things. So how will you be creative with what you have been given? How will you invest and collab with God with what he has entrusted to you?

When you collab with God, you get to make something truly meaningful. Truly beautiful. Something joyful, something rich with meaning, something funny, something passionate. Something wondrous.

You unlock your purpose by collaborating and creating with God.

And here's the good news: God wants to do it with you. Unlike the master in the parable, God hasn't given you talents and then left. In fact, he has promised the opposite. He made the same power available to you with your talents that Jesus had to rise from the dead.[105]

In other words, there's no excuse not to *imagine* with God.

---

105 Romans 8:11, NLT: "The Spirit of God, who raised Jesus from the dead, lives in you."

What if Moses had refused to put his hands up and raise the staff? What if he had thought, *My talent is stick-holding. That's no big deal. Holding up a stick isn't going to change the world, so why bother?*

What beauty can we create if we collaborate with God? What love can we spread? What joy? What restoration can we initiate?

What poetry? What art? What music? What performance? What acting? What dancing? What design? What engineering? What solution? What healing?

This is the best life possible.

God created.

God created you.

God created you to create.

God created you to create with him.

So nothing is impossible.

imaginate.

ABOUT THE AUTHORS

John Michael Hinton. Magician. Storyteller. Redhead. Driven by a passion to encourage people to embrace joy, he uses the power of magic, storytelling, and humor in a mix that you won't soon forget. As seen on the CW's hit show *Penn & Teller: Fool Us*, and with millions of views on YouTube, John Michael is a sought-after speaker and entertainer. When not traveling coast to coast, he spends his free time sharing large cups of black tea with his beautiful wife and playing with his three children. Outside of his family, his favorite things in life are cooking Italian food, a good suspenseful movie, and family trips to Disney World and NYC.

Ken Castor. After thirty years of next-generation work, Dr. Ken is balding but still bold. He is the Family and Next-Gen Pastor at Wooddale Church. He served as the Professor of Youth Ministry at Crown College for over a decade and in next-gen ministry for two decades before that. Ken helped create the award-winning *Jesus-Centered Bible* and has authored numerous discipleship resources like *Grow Down* and *Make a Difference*. He's also a nerdy Cubs fan, has several Chuck Taylors, and enjoys living in Minnesota with his brilliantly witty and slightly freezing family.